PIVOT POINT

PIVOT POINT FUNDAMENTALS: COSMETOLOGY
SCULPTURE/CUT

©1980-2021 Pivot Point International, Inc.
All rights reserved.
ISBN 978-1-940593-44-9

1st Edition
4th Printing, October 2021
Printed in China

Pivot Point International, Inc.
Global Headquarters
8725 West Higgins Road, Suite 700
Chicago, IL 60631 USA

847-866-0500
pivot-point.com

2

CONTENTS
105ᶜ // SCULPTURE/CUT

40

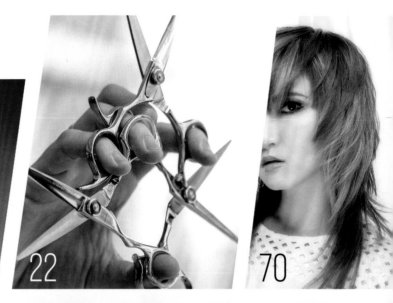

22

70

167

70

EXPLORE //
What do you consider the most
popular haircut for your generation?

Understanding the four basic forms and the techniques used to create them will prepare you to create any popular haircut.

Following this lesson on *Sculpture Theory,* you'll be able to:

ACHIEVE //

>> Identify the three levels of observation as related to hair sculpture

>> Describe the two ways to analyze the length arrangement of a hair sculpture

>> Illustrate the shape, texture and structure of the four basic forms

>> Classify combination forms within hair sculptures by the four basic forms

>> Evaluate the effects of different shapes and surface textures on the same client

FOCUS // **SCULPTURE THEORY**

Sculpture Transformation
Hair Sculpture Analysis
Four Basic Forms
Combination Forms
Change the Sculpture, Change the Effect

105°.1 | SCULPTURE THEORY

Hair sculpting is defined as the artistic carving or removing of hair lengths to create various forms and shapes. Just as a sculptor molds and carves clay into a work of art, a hair designer shapes a head of hair. Only the tools and the medium are different. Hair sculpting is also known as haircutting.

The number one service salon clients request is a haircut. This service is referred to as a sculpture or cut throughout this program. Hair sculptures are identified according to their length arrangement.

Hair sculptures often get labeled with names that attempt to reflect their forms or shapes. The length arrangement, called structure, produces the form. For example, when the length arrangement of hair is all one length, it's known as a uniformly layered form.

Uniformly Layered Form

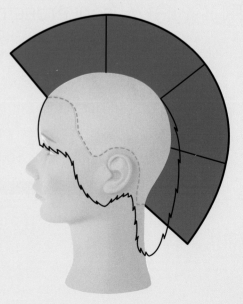

Uniformly Layered Structure

SCULPTURE TRANSFORMATION

Sculpture transformation is all about changing the shape (silhouette), the surface texture and the structure of a hair design.

Because the sculpture/cut is the foundation of all the other hair services, it is crucial that the fundamentals of hair sculpting become second nature to you. Without a good cut or sculpture, the overall design you and your client have in mind will be difficult for you to achieve and for the client to maintain.

When creating a sculpture for your client, communication is most important. All short hair is not the same, all medium-length hair is not the same and all long hair is not the same. Designers can identify the ways in which hair sculptures differ by analyzing the shape, position of weight or volume, texture, and length arrangement. Hair sculpting can:

BEFORE   AFTER

» **Stand alone as a core salon service**

» **Serve as the foundation for other services such as color or perm**

» **Create a dramatic change in the client's image**

 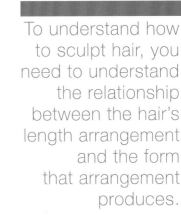

To understand how to sculpt hair, you need to understand the relationship between the hair's length arrangement and the form that arrangement produces.

HAIR SCULPTURE ANALYSIS

Hair can assume an infinite variety of forms such as differences in:

>> Shape
>> Texture
>> Structure

Hair sculpture analysis begins by using a consistent system of communication, which is based on "selective seeing" through the three levels of observation:

>> Basic
>> Detail
>> Abstract

Analyzing a hair sculpture using the levels of observation helps train your eye to gather information that will allow you to re-create what you see and inspire design adaptation.

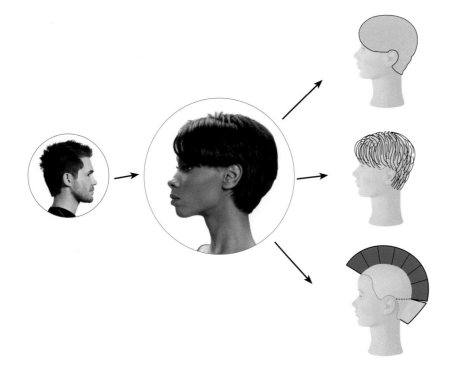

BASIC – FORM/SHAPE

>> Identify basic form or shape

>> Observe outer boundary or silhouette known as the **form line**

DETAIL – TEXTURE

>> Identify the detail in the texture or surface appearance

ABSTRACT – STRUCTURE

>> View hair as if it is standing straight out or projected at a 90° angle from the various curves of the head

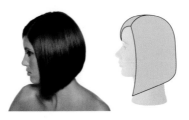

FORM/SHAPE

First, analyze the silhouette of the design, while blocking out any extraneous information, such as the texture or color.

TEXTURE

Second, look at the detail of the surface to identify the type of texture you see. There are two categories of surface appearance:

›› Unactivated: Smooth texture with smooth, unbroken lines

›› Activated: Rough texture with broken lines and exposed ends

STRUCTURE

Structure is defined as the arrangement of lengths across the curves of the head. The various length arrangements create the shape of a sculpted form.

Structure Graphic

›› Diagram that provides an abstract view of the length arrangement to scale and proportion
›› Serves as a blueprint for the final sculpture
›› Similar to the details of an architect's blueprint for a building

Two basic ways to analyze the structure of a hair sculpture:

›› **Natural fall**
›› **Normal projection**

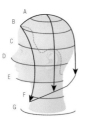

LEVELS

A - Apex
B - Hairline
C - Eye
D - Ear Lobe
E - Chin
F - Neck
G - Shoulder

Natural Fall

›› Describes the hair as the lengths lay or fall naturally over the curves of the head

›› Allows you to observe and analyze the texture of the hair, the direction and character of the form line and the overall shape

›› Describes the length or level to which the hair falls on the anatomy, such as the ear lobe, chin or neck

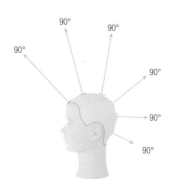

Normal Projection

›› Another way to analyze the structure or length arrangement of a hair sculpture

›› Hair is viewed abstractly as if it were projected at a 90° angle from the various curves of the head

SALON**CONNECTION**

It's All in a Name

A client may come into the salon and ask you for a haircut such as a "bob." Others will ask you for trendy haircuts, such as the "lob" which is a term made up of two words, long + bob. Other clients may ask you for a haircut made famous by a celebrity. You may even hear about the "wedge" or the "pixie." It is your responsibility to stay current with the trendy names a client might refer to when describing a haircut!

FOUR BASIC FORMS

There are four basic forms that, when used alone or in any combination, make up all hair designs. Each form has a unique shape, structure and texture and each can be sculpted at a variety of lengths.

The four basic forms are:

1. Solid form
2. Graduated form
3. Increase-layered form
4. Uniformly layered form

Each form is described in this section along with its color-coded structure graphic.

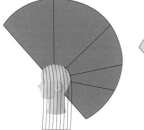

Solid Form

Graduated Form

Increase-Layered Form

Uniformly Layered Form

The shape of a hair sculpture is largely determined by where the weight is positioned. **Weight** is created by the concentration of length within a given area. Understanding how to work with weight allows you to reposition the amount of expansion within a design, changing its shape to better suit the client.

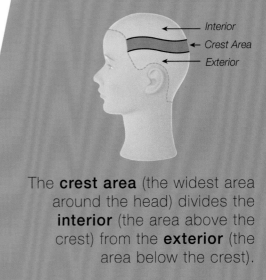

Interior
← Crest Area
→ Exterior

The **crest area** (the widest area around the head) divides the **interior** (the area above the crest) from the **exterior** (the area below the crest).

SOLID FORM

The **solid form** consists of lengths that progress from shorter in the exterior to longer in the interior.

>> In natural fall, all lengths fall to one level, resulting in an unbroken, unactivated surface texture.

>> Near the top, the shape echoes the curves of the head; at the bottom, the shape reflects the buildup of weight at the perimeter.

>> Sometimes referred to as a one-length cut, bob, Dutch boy, blunt cut or 0° angle cut.

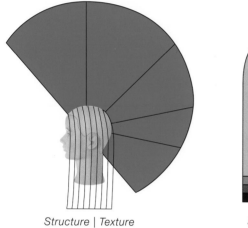

Structure | Texture

Shape | Weight

Color-Coded: Blue

Shape: Rectangle

Texture: Unactivated

Structure: Shorter exterior progressing to longer interior

Weight: Maximum weight develops at the form line since all lengths fall to the same level

2

GRADUATED
FORM

GRADUATED FORM

The **graduated form** consists of shorter exterior lengths that gradually progress toward longer interior lengths.

» In natural fall, the ends appear to stack up along an angle, resulting in a combination of unactivated texture in the interior and activated texture in the exterior.

» The line that divides the two textures is known as a ridge line.

» Weight occurs above the perimeter form line, creating the visual impression of a triangular shape.

» Sometimes referred to as a wedge or 45° angle cut.

Structure | Texture

Shape | Weight

Color-Coded: Yellow

Shape: Triangle

Texture: Unactivated/Activated

Structure: Shorter exterior gradually progressing to longer interior

Weight: Found above the perimeter form line, where the unactivated and activated textures meet

INCREASE-LAYERED FORM

The **increase-layered** form consists of shorter interior lengths that progress toward longer exterior lengths.

>> In natural fall, this progression creates a totally activated surface texture with no visible weight.

>> Because the lengths of hair are dispersed across the curves of the head, the increase-layered form generally has an elongated or oval shape.

>> Sometimes referred to as a shag or 180° angle cut.

Structure | Texture

Shape | Weight

Color-Coded: Red

Shape: Oval

Texture: Activated

Structure: Shorter interior progressing to longer exterior

Weight: No concentration of weight since lengths disperse across the curves of the head

3

INCREASE-LAYERED FORM

4

UNIFORMLY
LAYERED
FORM

UNIFORMLY LAYERED FORM

The **uniformly layered form** consists of the same lengths throughout the design.

» In natural fall, the repetition of lengths produces a totally activated texture with no discernible weight.

» Lengths disperse over the curves of the head, creating a rounded shape that follows the curves of the head.

» Sometimes referred to as a layered cut or 90° angle cut.

Structure | Texture

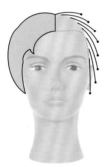

Shape | Weight

Color-Coded: Green

Shape: Circular

Texture: Activated

Structure: Same length throughout

Weight: No concentration of weight since lengths disperse across the curves of the head

MEN

The four basic forms and their individual characteristics apply to both the female and male client. Although not considered a fifth form, **gradation**–also color-coded yellow–is a very short version of the graduated form. With gradation, shorter exterior lengths gradually progress to longer interior lengths and are generally combined with other forms. Fades and bald fades are examples of gradation.

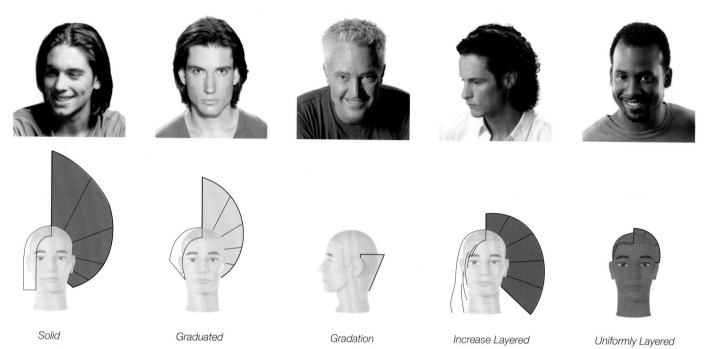

| Solid | Graduated | Gradation | Increase Layered | Uniformly Layered |

COMBINATION FORMS

A large percentage of the designs that you will create for your clients will consist of **combination forms**, which include two or more of the four basic forms within a sculpture. The properties of the four basic forms can be combined in an infinite number of ways to create designs that are perfectly suited for each individual client.

The proportional relationship of each form within a combination produces the shape, texture and position of weight in the final design.

INCREASE/SOLID

When an increase-layered interior is combined with a solid exterior, the illusion of an activated surface appearance is achieved while maintaining maximum perimeter weight.

INCREASE/UNIFORM/GRADATION

Gradated exterior lengths create a close-fitting contour that blends with the uniformly layered lengths, while the increase-layered fringe elongates the form and creates height and fullness.

UNIFORM/GRADUATED

In this uniform-graduated combination, shorter exterior lengths progressively blend to uniformly layered interior lengths creating a totally activated surface texture.

UNIFORM/INCREASE

Uniform interior lengths are combined with increase-layered exterior lengths for a highly activated surface and elongation toward the perimeter.

GRADUATION/UNIFORM/GRADATION

Gradation creates a close-fitting exterior and blends to uniformly layered lengths, creating a rounded interior. Graduated interior lengths create weight to achieve a focal point toward the face.

SQUARE (RECTILINEAR) FORM

In this combination form, a weight area is created where the increase-layered form meets the graduated form, resulting in a square form.

Square Form – Hair: Andrzej Matracki, Photography: Sylwia Sokolowska, Model: Marcin Wydych

CHANGE THE SCULPTURE, CHANGE THE EFFECT

With your training as a hair designer you will have the power to transform your clients' appearance. A change in hair sculpture can transform a client's look in any number of ways—becoming more sporty, more sophisticated, more professional or more cutting-edge. Notice the changes created by sculpting the hair into different shapes and surface textures, and the effects these changes have on each client in the examples shown here.

DISCOVER**MORE**

Iconic Haircuts
Did you know that many trends are inspired from popular haircuts from the past? Search the Internet for iconic haircuts that set trends in your generation and share your favorites with your classmates.

Using the four basic forms individually, or in any combination, will allow you to break down and adapt any hair sculpture that your client requests and compose your own unique designs—even setting trends.

LESSONS LEARNED

» The three levels of observation are basic (form/shape), detail (texture) and abstract (structure).

» The two ways to analyze the structure of a hair sculpture are in natural fall and normal projection.

» The four basic forms are: solid form, graduated form, increase-layered form and uniformly layered form.

BASIC FORM	STRUCTURE/ TEXTURE	SHAPE/ WEIGHT
SOLID FORM		
GRADUATED FORM		
INCREASE-LAYERED FORM		
UNIFORMLY LAYERED FORM		

» Various forms within combination forms can be identified by the four basic forms.

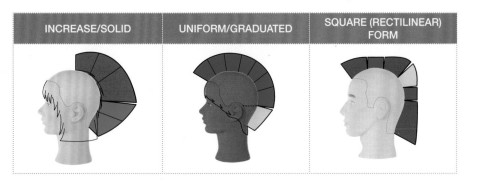

INCREASE/SOLID	UNIFORM/GRADUATED	SQUARE (RECTILINEAR) FORM

» Different shapes and surface textures can affect the client's appearance.

INCREASE/SOLID	UNIFORM/GRADUATED	UNIFORM/GRADATION

Do you think the quality of a tool reflects the price you pay for the tool? Why?

INSPIRE //

From creating clean, blunt lines to soft, wispy textures —the choice of tools and products is up to you.

ACHIEVE //

Following this lesson on *Sculpture Tools and Essentials*, you'll be able to:

>> Describe the function of the five main sculpting tools
>> Provide examples of supplies, products and equipment used to perform a hair sculpture

FOCUS //
SCULPTURE TOOLS AND ESSENTIALS

Shears
Taper Shears
Razors
Clippers
Combs
Sculpting Essentials

Sculpture tools are the hand-held tools (implements) used for cutting hair. Because different tools have different effects on the hair, the tools you choose will impact the final result. Each tool allows subtle variations in texture, particularly at the form line. Through the design decision process, you will determine the form to be sculpted and the appropriate tool to use. Being familiar with each tool will enable you to make the proper selections for the desired results.

Sculpting tools require disinfection after each use. Follow your area's regulatory agency's guidelines for infection control.

The five tools most often used to sculpt hair are:

- » Shears

- » Taper shears

- » Razors

- » Clippers

- » Combs

These tools—together with proper techniques—produce all salon sculptures.

SHEARS

Shears, also called straight shears, produce a clean, blunt edge. By varying the position of the shears as you sculpt, you can create subtle to dramatic variations in the hairstrand.

Shears are the primary tool used for hair sculpting. As with every tool, shears are an investment. Select a quality pair and care for them as you would any fine instrument. Shears come in many different styles and lengths and are made from a variety of materials, ranging from porcelain to cobalt steel.

>> Blade lengths range from as short as 4" (10 cm) to as long as 7½" (18.75 cm).

>> Short shears are generally used for more precision or detailed sculpting.

>> Longer shears are used for overcomb techniques and for sculpting larger sections of hair.

It is important to properly maintain your shears.

>> Wipe off blades with a soft cloth and disinfect your shears after every service.

>> Add several drops of oil to the inner pivot area and then open and close shears several times.

>> Have shears professionally sharpened when needed.

>> Never sculpt or cut anything with your shears other than hair to avoid dulling your blades prematurely.

DISCOVER**MORE**

Tools of the Trade
Shears are a big investment. Did you know that you could spend anywhere from $50 to $1,000 or more on a good pair of shears? Take good care of them. Avoid dropping them on the floor because that could nick and misalign blades. Routine maintenance will greatly prolong shear life and keep them working at peak performance. Search the Internet to compare various types of shears, including different materials and prices.

PARTS OF THE SHEARS

A pair of shears consists of two blades:

» A still or stationary blade, which is controlled by the finger grip

» A movable, or action blade, which is controlled by the thumb grip

The two blades are joined by the tension or hand screw. The thumb and finger grips may be even with each other or they may be offset. Some shears have a finger brace on which the small finger rests for comfort and balance. The finger brace may or may not be removable.

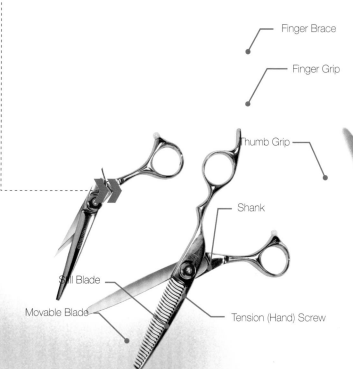

Finger Brace

Finger Grip

Thumb Grip

Shank

Still Blade

Movable Blade

Tension (Hand) Screw

HOW TO HOLD THE SHEARS AND COMB

Being comfortable with your tools is the first step to overcoming any concerns you may have about hair sculpting, so it is important to learn how to hold them properly.

Insert Ring Finger

Insert Thumb

Remove Thumb and Palm Shears

An Alternative Method
Palm Shears

Hold Comb

Insert your ring or third finger into the finger grip to control the still blade.

Insert the tip of your thumb into the thumb grip to control the movable blade. Note that placing more of your thumb into the thumb grip lessens the amount of control you have. Place your index and middle fingers on top of the shears for greater control. Rest your little finger on the finger brace if your shears have one.

When combing the hair or making a parting during a hair sculpture, it is necessary to hold the comb and shears in the same hand. To do this without jeopardizing your client's safety, palm your shears by releasing your thumb from the thumb grip and closing your palm over the shears.

Rest the blade of the shears on the outside of the palm.

Hold the comb between your thumb and index finger of the same hand. Once the hair is distributed (combed), transfer the comb to the opposite hand for sculpting.

SCULPTING POSITIONS

The sculpting position you choose will depend on the area of the head you're working on, the desired results and how comfortable the position is for you. In most cases, you will work with finger, shear and shoulder positions that are parallel. Some common sculpting positions include: palm down, palm up (or out), palm-to-palm and on top of the fingers.

Palm Down
Position the palm of your sculpting hand downward.

Palm Up
Position the palm of your sculpting hand upward.

Palm-to-Palm
When sculpting graduated lengths, the hair is held away from the head. Position the palm of your sculpting hand so that it faces the palm of your other hand.

On Top of the Fingers
In most cases you will sculpt under, or inside, your fingers as shown in the previous photo. When lifting the lengths on top of the head, however, you will need to sculpt the hair along the top of your fingers.

When sculpting against the skin or to refine a perimeter, the hand may be positioned toward the head with the still blade against the skin.

TAPER SHEARS

Taper shears, also known as thinning or texturizing shears, consist of one straight blade and one notched (serrated) blade. They produce a distinct and regular alternation of shorter and longer lengths. Taper shears with more, closely spaced teeth will remove a greater amount of hair. Taper shears with fewer, widely spaced teeth will remove less hair.

>> Used for creating shorter lengths within the form or on the ends of the hair to reduce bulk and create mobility

>> One blade of the taper shears is straight and the other is notched (serrated)

>> Purpose of the notches is to hold the hair; as the blade closes, only the hair held in the notches will be sculpted; the remaining hair will be pushed between the teeth and remain at the original length

>> Distance between the notches (teeth) of the taper shear blade will determine the amount of hair that will be sculpted and/or the degree of taper

>> Can be used on damp or dry hair

>> Require disinfection; follow manufacturer's directions and disinfection guidelines

PARTS OF THE TAPER SHEARS

Taper shears have the same parts as shears except, as mentioned before, instead of having two straight-edge blades, taper shears have one straight-edge blade and one notched blade.

>> The notched blade has teeth that are spaced at different intervals.

>> Taper shears are held the same way as shears.

Finger Brace

Finger Grip

Tension (Hand) Screw

Shank

Movable
Straight-Edge
Blade

Still Notched Blade

Thumb Grip

TYPES OF TAPER SHEARS

Each manufacturer labels their taper–or texturizing–shears by the number of teeth along the blade. Samples are shown here.

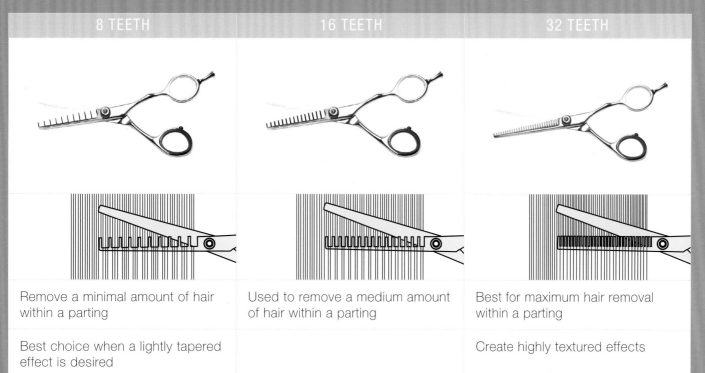

8 TEETH	16 TEETH	32 TEETH
Remove a minimal amount of hair within a parting	Used to remove a medium amount of hair within a parting	Best for maximum hair removal within a parting
Best choice when a lightly tapered effect is desired		Create highly textured effects

CHANNELING SHEARS

Channeling shears have wider notches that produce dramatic chunky effects. Channeling shears are primarily used for special effects such as extreme length variations and heavy fringes or notched perimeter lengths.

RAZORS

A **razor** produces tapering or an angled effect on the end of each strand, which results in more mobility and a softer, somewhat diffused form line.

>> Tapering may occur on the top or bottom of the strand, depending on the sculpting technique you use.

>> The razor may be used to sculpt the entire form or to texturize within the form.

There are a variety of razors available to the professional hair designer that suit different styles of sculpting and levels of comfort.

Typical features may include:

>> The ability to fold

>> A guard that is used over the blade for protection or for texturizing techniques

>> Blade made from high-quality surgical steel

>> Soft, flexible steel blade

When sculpting with a razor, it is essential that the hair be damp throughout. If the hair is too dry, sculpting will be more difficult and possibly uncomfortable for the client.

PARTS OF THE RAZOR

The razor consists of a blade and usually a guard, which is used to protect you from coming in direct contact with the edge of the blade. The shank is used to hold the razor, while the handle, which is sometimes foldable, is used to rest your fingers. The tang is used to rest the little finger.

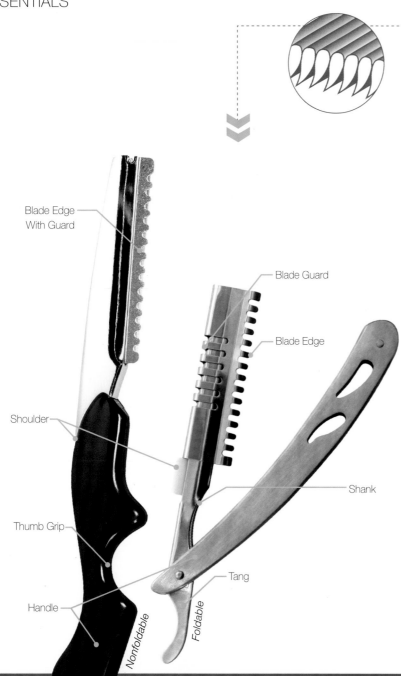

Blade Edge With Guard

Blade Guard

Blade Edge

Shoulder

Shank

Thumb Grip

Handle

Tang

Nonfoldable

Foldable

IMPORTANT SAFETY TIPS FOR USING A RAZOR

>> Use the razor on damp-to-wet hair for the comfort of the client and ease in sculpting.

>> Use a guard when applicable.

>> Disinfect your razor before and after every service using general disinfection guidelines.

>> Read manufacturer's directions before changing the blade.

>> Replace the blade when it becomes dull.

>> Check with your area's regulating agency to determine whether you may remove nape or sideburn hair with a razor.

>> Use extreme caution when sculpting around moles, scars and skin lesions.

>> Discard used razor blades in a puncture-proof or sharps container.

How to Hold the Razor

There are several ways you can hold the razor. The descriptions that follow explain how to hold a foldable razor and a nonfoldable razor.

With a foldable razor, the handle is generally positioned straight out, or flat while you are sculpting. Position your thumb at the bottom of the shank and position the rest of your fingers on top of the shank.

You can also bend the handle upward and rest your little finger on the tang. This is helpful when sculpting in tight areas, such as around the perimeter hairline.

When working with a nonfoldable razor, position your thumb in the thumb groove and position your remaining fingers on top of the razor. This hand position works well when using texturizing techniques along a section of hair.

As an alternative, you can position your index finger on top of the razor while holding the razor with your thumb and remaining fingers. This hand position allows greater flexibility.

Removing and Inserting the Razor Blade

Removing

>> Carefully remove the guard by first tightly grasping the razor handle and shank with the sculpting edge pointing upward, and then carefully slide the guard toward the end of the shank.

>> Push the blade out using the guard. Place the flat side of the guard against the shank, with the razor blade positioned between the teeth of the guard.

Inserting

>> Hold the razor handle and shank with the blade slot directed upward.

>> Grasp the razor blade with the sculpting edge pointing upward.

>> Align the blade with the blade slot, and insert the blade into the blade slot until it is secure.

>> Position the outer edge of the blade between two teeth of the razor guard. Notice the teeth are locked into position in the blade slot. Maintain constant pressure and firmly push the blade into the full slot position.

Razor Dispenser

Some razors come with a razor blade dispenser, which makes replacing razor blades safer and easier. Simply use the dispenser to slide on the new blade once the old one has been removed. Discard the old blade in a puncture-proof container.

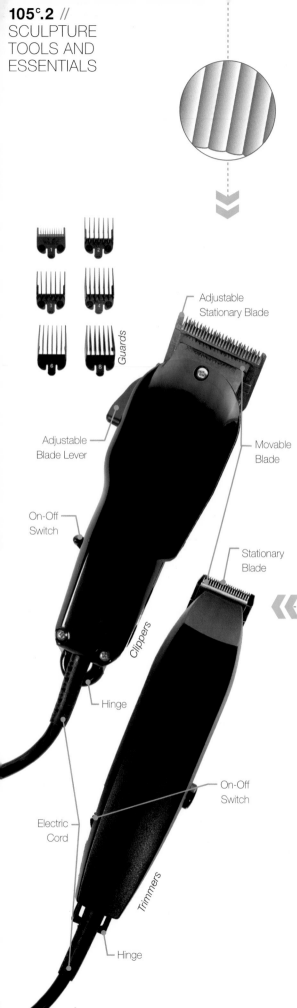

CLIPPERS

Clippers are an electric tool that can achieve a variety of effects, depending on the blade attachment–or guard–used. Clippers can be used, for example, to create clean, precise lines or a soft, broom-like effect.

Clippers are generally chosen to quickly sculpt larger sections of hair. Some clippers come with attachments called guards, which range from ⅛" (0.3 cm) to 1" (2.5 cm). These guards enable you to consistently sculpt the hair at the same length as the size of the guard. For instance, a ⅛" (0.3 cm) guard will sculpt the hair ⅛" (0.3 cm) from the scalp.

When extremely short lengths are desired, no guard is used.

Another way to determine and vary the distance from the scalp while sculpting is the clipper-over-comb technique. With this technique the clippers are positioned on top of the comb while sculpting.

Trimmers

Small clippers, known as trimmers or edgers, are used to outline and refine the hairline, beard, mustache and sideburn areas.

PARTS OF THE CLIPPERS

» The stationary blade of the clippers, also called the heel, is similar in function to the stationary blade of the shears.

» The movable blade moves in a side-to-side motion as it sculpts the hair.

» The adjustable blade lever is used to adjust the stationary blade.

» Some clippers have an electrical cord while others are cordless.

» A stiff-bristle clipper brush is used to clean the tool after each use.

» Blades should be removed for cleaning. Do not clean the clippers while they are turned on.

» The detachable blade and heel should be disinfected between clients. Many professionals use a spray disinfectant.

» Clipper oil provides lubrication for the moving parts of the tool to keep them in good working condition, but should be used sparingly.

» Read manufacturer's directions for cleaning guidelines.

Blade Attachments

Blade attachments are available in different lengths and widths to achieve a variety of results that range from removing large sections of hair to lining and precision detailed work. Shown below are blades designed for detachable clipper systems.

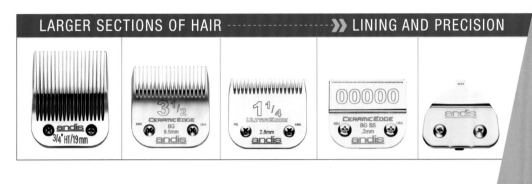

HOW TO HOLD THE CLIPPERS

The clippers can be held in a number of different ways, depending on the area of the head, the line or angle sculpted and your comfort level.

One way to hold the clippers is to position your palm over them and position your thumb on the side.

Another way to hold the clippers is to position your thumb on top of them and position your remaining fingers underneath.

ALERT!
Never use clipper blades that have broken teeth, and always align a new set of blades.

SALON**CONNECTION**

Stay Current, Learn About New Tools
Salon professionals generally own their own tools and make investment decisions according to their awareness of what is available and their personal preference. Manufacturers continuously offer new options to classic tool design. New tools are often driven by advancements in quality construction and ergonomic features. When you are ready to purchase new tools, ask industry friends about their favorites, research information online, and "try before you buy" at trade shows.

COMBS

A comb is used to distribute and control the hair before and during sculpting. The amount of space between the teeth of the comb is very important in determining which comb best suits your purpose.

>> The wider the spaces are between the teeth of the comb, the less tension is placed on the hair before or during sculpting. This results in softer finished lines.

>> Closely spaced teeth will ribbon the hair more, allowing you to sculpt very precise lines.

Various comb sizes and shapes are used to control the hair. In particular, the main differences in combs are the sizes of the teeth, the spaces between the teeth and the desired results.

Shampoo Comb	Master Sketcher	Cutting Comb	Taper Comb Contour/Barber Comb
Designed to detangle wet hair in preparation for a hair sculpture	Used for controlling or distributing larger amounts of hair	Consists of both fine and wide teeth	Allows you to sculpt as close to the scalp as possible while using shear-over-comb and clipper-over-comb techniques
	Used with clipper-over-comb and shear-over-comb techniques	Used for distribution when working with medium-sized sections of hair	

SCULPTING TOOLS

The following chart summarizes the tools and their related functions.

TOOLS	FUNCTION
Shears	Provide a clean, blunt edge or line
Taper Shears	Create a distinct and regular alternation of shorter and longer lengths for mobility
Razor	Creates a tapered effect on edge of each strand, which produces a softer, somewhat diffused line
Clippers	Create clean, precise lines or a soft, broom-like effect; various blade attachments (guards) allow hair to be sculpted at various distances from scalp
Trimmers	Used to outline hairline, beard and sideburns
Shampoo Comb	Detangles wet hair in preparation for hair sculpture
Master Sketcher Comb	Controls and distributes larger amounts of hair; also used for overcomb techniques
Cutting Comb	Parts and distributes hair; primary comb for sculpting and overcomb techniques
Taper/Barber Comb	Helps sculpt short lengths and refine perimeter when used against skin

SCULPTING ESSENTIALS

The following charts will help you become familiar with the various supplies, products and equipment you will use in the salon.

>> Hair sculpting supplies include disposable items such as neck strips and reusable items such as towels, capes and water bottles.

>> Hair sculpting products range in viscosity from liquids to solids that can be used throughout the hair sculpting service.

>> Hair sculpting equipment includes the furnishings, such as the shampoo bowl, necessary for a professional sculpting service.

Keep in mind that Safety Data Sheets (SDS) for all products used in the salon are required to be available in the salon for your review.

SCULPTING SUPPLIES

SUPPLIES	FUNCTION
Towel	Protects client from getting wet during shampoo service
Plastic Cape	Protects client's clothing during shampoo and hair sculpting service
Cloth Cape	Protects client's clothing during dry hair sculpting service
Neck Strip	Protects client's skin from contact with cape; replaces towel during hair sculpting service
Spray Bottle	Holds water; used to keep hair damp while sculpting

SCULPTING PRODUCTS

PRODUCTS	FUNCTION
Sculpting Lotion	Controls hair while sculpting
Gel	Creates wet-look finishes
Mousse	Defines texture; creates light hold to firm hold on wet or dry hair
Pomade	Adds gloss and sheen to dry hair; creates texture separation; also referred to as polisher, glosser, lusterizer and brilliantine

SCULPTING EQUIPMENT

EQUIPMENT	FUNCTION
Hair Sculpting Station	Provides a place for tools to be displayed and organized
Hydraulic Chair	Provides proper back support for client during hair sculpting service; adjustable
Disinfectant Container	Holds solution for disinfecting tools
Shampoo Bowl	Supports client's neck and holds water and shampoo products during shampoo service

Understanding the various effects achieved from a variety of sculpting tools enables you to safely, skillfully and artistically create the desired effects for your clients.

LESSONS LEARNED

The five main sculpting tools and their function include:

>> Shears – Produce a clean blunt edge

>> Taper or Texturizing Shears – Produce a distinct and regular alternation of shorter and longer lengths

>> Razor – Produces tapering or an angle effect on the end of each strand

>> Clippers – Electric implement that creates clean, precise lines to soft, broom-like effects

>> Combs:
>>   Shampoo Comb – detangles hair
>>   Master Sketcher – controls larger amounts of hair
>>   Cutting Comb – used to distribute hair
>>   Taper/Barber Comb – used to sculpt close to the scalp

In addition to the sculpting tools, sculpting essentials include the supplies, products and equipment that are needed to perform a hair sculpting service:

>> Supplies include towels, plastic and cloth capes, spray bottles and neck strips.

>> Sculpting products include sculpting lotion, gel, mousse and pomade.

>> Equipment includes permanent fixtures such as the hair sculpting station, hydraulic chair and shampoo bowl.

105°.3 //
SCULPTURE SKILLS

EXPLORE //

Why do you think a haircut can cost $10 at one salon and $100 at another salon?

INSPIRE //

Pivot Point's proven 7 Sculpting Procedures will help you create consistent, impressive and predictable results.

ACHIEVE //

Following this lesson on *Sculpture Skills*, you'll be able to:

>> State the 7 Sculpting Procedures in the sequential order they are used to perform a hair sculpture

>> Describe each of the 7 Sculpting Procedures

>> List additional factors to consider when sculpting hair

FOCUS //

SCULPTURE SKILLS

The 7 Sculpting Procedures

Sculpting Considerations

105ᶜ.3 | SCULPTURE SKILLS

Did you know that one of the most common reasons why clients don't return to the same designer is that their hair was cut too short? When you think about it, a color that's too light can be darkened, an updo the client doesn't like can be redone, but a haircut that is too short needs time to grow out.

Following the 7 Sculpting Procedures allows you to create the hair sculpture that you have visualized and designed with your client.

DISCOVER**MORE**

Predict Your Results! Success in most things is based on following a tried-and-true sequence of steps. Remember when you learned how to drive a car or make your favorite recipe? Each step was deliberate and thoughtful. The more often you repeated the sequence, the more second nature it became, and the more predictable your result. Think of the 7 Sculpting Procedures as your recipe for haircutting success: the most logical way to create and duplicate hair sculptures.

THE 7 SCULPTING PROCEDURES

The 7 Sculpting Procedures are a unique system for producing predictable sculpture results. Developing your technical skills and following systematic sculpting procedures will allow you to achieve accuracy and consistency in all of your work. The 7 Sculpting Procedures are:

7 SCULPTING PROCEDURES

| 1. Section | 2. Head Position | 3. Part | 4. Distribute |

| 5. Project | 6. Finger/Shear Position | 7. Design Line |

SECTION (1)

Many successful hair sculptures begin with sectioning and dividing the hair into workable areas for control, called **sections**. Generally, sectioning is performed with the wide-tooth end of the sculpting comb, and individual sections are kept neat and secured with clips. One common sectioning pattern divides the hair into four sections by parting from the center front hairline to the nape, and from the apex to each ear. The numbers of sections and the types of sectioning patterns you choose depend on the type of hair sculpture you will be creating.

Sectioning is determined by:

- Changes in design lines, projection angles or distribution

- Hair's natural growth patterns

- Each form's proportional relationship within the combination form

The most common terms used to identify the reference points of the head are:

- **Apex** – Top or highest point of head

- **Crest Area** – Widest area of the head

- **Interior** – Area above the crest area

- **Exterior** – Area below the crest area

- **Front** and **Back** – Divided by a line that runs from the apex to each ear

- **Top** – Upper portion of scalp, behind the forehead

- **Side** – Area in front of and above the ear

- **Fringe Area** – Area in front of the apex that may extend to the outer corner of each eye

- **Crown** – Area in the upper back and on top of the crest area, begins where the top of the head begins to curve downward

- **Occipital** – Protruding bone located below the crest area in back of the head

- **Nape** – Area below the occipital

- **Perimeter** – Area all around the hairline

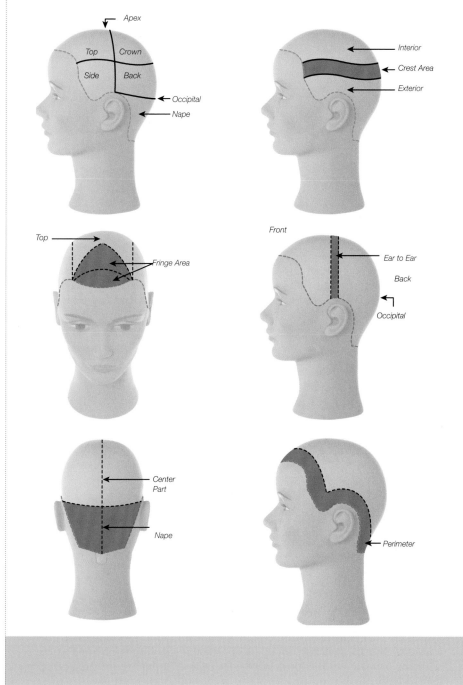

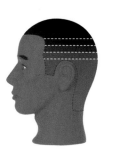

Sometimes hair may be too short to section effectively. That's when designers envision zones within the sculpted form. The zones act as sections do, separating between different techniques and design lines.

HEAD POSITION (2)

The **head position**—upright, forward or tilted to either side—directly influences the fall of the hair, which affects the texture and the direction of the sculpted line. You will usually want the head position to remain constant while sculpting a given area to maintain consistency.

Upright

The upright head position is most frequently used to achieve the most natural, pure result. Sculpting the hair with the head in an upright position allows the designer to see the natural fall of the hair and more clearly distinguish the design line and projection angles.

Forward

When the head is in a forward position, the neck is stretched. Sculpting with the head in this position produces hair lengths that are slightly shorter in the nape and longer surface lengths. This results in a slight underbevel effect with ends that turn under when the head is returned to its normal upright position.

Tilting the client's head forward is often used when refining form lines or when sculpting the nape area very short. This position is also commonly used when sculpting increase-layered forms since it facilitates distributing and projecting the lengths upward.

Tilted

The head may be tilted to one side or the other to refine form lines. When sculpting short forms, designers may choose to tilt the client's head toward either side in order to refine the hairline at the ear and sideburn area or to refine the form line at the sides.

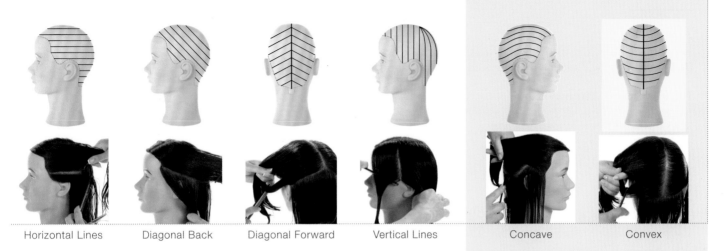

Horizontal Lines | Diagonal Back | Diagonal Forward | Vertical Lines | Concave | Convex

Partings are lines that subdivide sections of hair in order to separate, distribute and control the hair while sculpting. For maximum ease, efficiency and precision when making partings, the hair is combed in the direction that the parting will be made.

>> The parting pattern used is generally parallel to the design line

>> The size of the parting, or the space between the parting lines is determined by the density of the hair

>> Diagonal-back lines are lines that travel away from the face, resulting in a backward flow of hair

>> Diagonal-forward lines are lines that travel toward the face, resulting in a forward flow of hair

Concave lines curve inward, like the inside of a sphere, while **convex** lines curve outward, like the outside of a sphere.

The **celestial axis** is a symbol used to identify straight and curved lines, directions and projection angles.

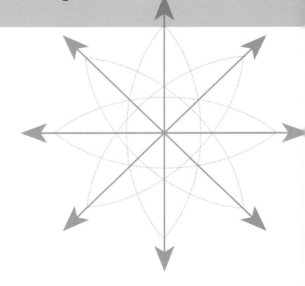

DISTRIBUTE (4)

Distribution is the direction the hair is combed in relation to its base parting.

The four types of distribution are:

>> Natural
>> Perpendicular
>> Shifted
>> Directional

NATURAL DISTRIBUTION	PERPENDICULAR DISTRIBUTION	SHIFTED DISTRIBUTION	DIRECTIONAL DISTRIBUTION
>> Direction hair assumes as it falls naturally from the head due to gravity >> Used from horizontal and diagonal partings >> Primarily used for solid form	>> Hair is combed at a 90°, or right angle from its base parting >> Used from horizontal, diagonal or vertical partings >> Primarily used to sculpt graduated and layered forms	>> Hair is combed out of natural distribution in any direction except perpendicular to its base parting; also known as overdirection >> Used from horizontal, diagonal and vertical partings >> Used when sculpting most forms, except solid form to achieve an exaggerated length increase and blending within the form	>> Hair is distributed straight up, straight out or straight back from the curve of the head >> Used from horizontal, vertical and diagonal partings >> Results in length increases due to the curve of the head; used to sculpt square (rectilinear) forms using the planar sculpting technique Planar sculpting is a technique in which the hair is sculpted along horizontal and vertical planes.

PROJECT (5)

Projection, also known as elevation, is the angle at which the hair is held in relation to the curve of the head prior to and while sculpting. The most common projection angles used in hair sculpting are 0°, 45° and 90°. Projecting below 90° builds weight. Projection angles 90° and above layer the hair and diminish weight. The higher the projection, the less weight buildup in the resulting form. A quadrant of the celestial axis is used to determine projection angles from the straight and curved surfaces of the head. Once 0° has been established, 45° and 90° angles can be determined in any direction.

Projection angles can also be identified within a range such as:

» Low Projection – 0°-30°

» Medium Projection – 30°-60°

» High Projection – 60°-90°

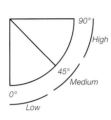

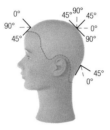

Projection for Solid Form

Natural fall is the natural position hair assumes due to gravitational pull. In some areas of the head, natural fall may also be 0°. When the hair is in natural fall, it is neither lifted from the scalp nor moved toward the scalp.

With 0° projection the hair is held flat to the surface of the head while sculpting.

Projection for Graduated Form

The standard projection angle used to sculpt graduated forms is 45°. The higher the projection angle, the greater the amount of graduated texture.

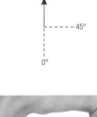

Projection for Increase-Layered Form

When sculpting increase-layered forms, the projection angle of the stationary design line establishes the location where all other lengths are converged. You will generally use a projection angle of either 0°, 45° or 90° for the stationary design line.

Projection for Uniformly Layered Form

The projection angle used to sculpt uniformly layered forms is 90° from the curve of the head. This is also called normal projection. Maintaining a consistent 90° angle from the various curves of the head is important for uniformly layered forms since inconsistency will result in uneven lengths.

FINGER/SHEAR POSITION (6)

Finger/shear position refers to the position of the fingers and the shears relative to the base parting. The two basic types of finger/shear position are parallel and nonparallel.

Parallel Finger/Shear Position

With a **parallel finger/shear position**, the fingers are positioned at an equal distance away from the parting while sculpting. Sculpting in this manner will result in the purest reflection of the chosen line. Since the shears will follow the fingers, this is also known as parallel sculpting.

Nonparallel Finger/Shear Position

With a **nonparallel finger/shear position**, the fingers are positioned unequally away from the parting while sculpting. This position is used to create exaggerated length increases, to blend between contrasting lengths.

DESIGN LINE (7)

A **design line** is the artistic pattern or length guide used while sculpting and can be stationary or mobile. Any straight or curved line of the celestial axis can be used to create or analyze a design line.

The design line may also be the perimeter form line, as in the solid form.

Stationary Design Line

A **stationary design line** is the constant, stationary guide to which all lengths are directed. This design line is used when a progression of lengths in the opposite direction is desired. A stationary design line is most often used to sculpt solid and increase-layered forms, and is used to achieve a weight area in graduated forms.

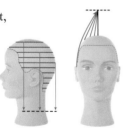

Mobile Design Line

A **mobile design line** is a movable guide that consists of a small amount of previously sculpted hair used as a length guide to sculpt subsequent partings. A mobile design line, sometimes called a traveling guide, is used to sculpt graduated and layered forms and square combination forms.

Cross-Checking

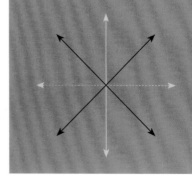

stage in sculpting, in which the balance and accuracy of the sculpture is checked by using the line opposite the original parting pattern. For example, when sculpting vertically, you cross-check horizontally. Cross-checking may be performed periodically throughout the service. If unwanted lengths are found, they should be sculpted with the original parting pattern used to sculpt the form.

Sculpting Skills for Today and Tomorrow

This lesson sets the foundation of a logical, yet creative approach to the skills needed to re-create the classic designs in this program. Even more important to you, this foundation will enable you to compose your own designs and create trends you see in the future. Knowing the rules and why they were established allows you to know when you can bend the rules, and what the result will be if you do.

SCULPTING CONSIDERATIONS

There are important considerations that serve to check your work and enhance the final results. For example, considering the client's natural growth patterns to determine which hair sculpture will work best and how to personalize that form are important steps that lead to client satisfaction. The sculpting considerations described in this section are:

>> Growth patterns
>> Fringe and nape variations
>> Curly hair considerations

GROWTH PATTERNS

You will need to adapt your sculpting techniques to accommodate natural growth patterns. These growth patterns are determined by the angle and direction at which the hair grows out of the scalp. Strong patterns may cause the hair to "stand up" if sculpted too short. Natural parts may influence the overall design proportions and symmetry.

When sculpting very short lengths, it's often recommended to work against the growth patterns while refining. This technique is most often performed on dry hair so that growth patterns are more obvious.

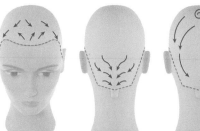

WIDOW'S PEAK	COWLICK	WHORL

Prominent hair growth pattern that forms from a point at the front hairline and curves to one side	Characterized by a strong growth pattern that moves to the right or left; usually found in straight or wavy hair at the front hairline or crown	Strong circular directional growth on either side of the nape or crown
Leave the fringe area longer to avoid a spiking effect with the hair sticking straight up	Sculpt the hair following the same direction it naturally grows and falls	Allow additional length so the hair will remain flat or sculpt the hair very close to the scalp to avoid spiking
	Allow additional length in this area to avoid spiking	

FRINGE AND NAPE VARIATIONS

The fringe is the hair that partially or completely covers the forehead in a hair design. The nape is the hair that covers the area at the back of the neck. It is important to adapt the fringe to the shape and features of your client's face. Likewise, consider the length and width of your client's neck when determining the right nape design.

Here are a few examples:

A layered fringe adds texture, fullness and height.

A longer fringe can be swept to the side to expose the forehead.

A solid fringe can frame the eyes.

Nape variations can be customized according to the hair's growth patterns and the dimensions of the client's neck and shoulders.

CURLY HAIR CONSIDERATIONS

The sculpting techniques that you have learned so far can be applied to straight or curly hair. However, when sculpting curly hair, there are some particular techniques that will help you create the desired result. Prior to sculpting curly hair, consider how the hair will be worn.

If the hair will be worn straight, you may wish to shampoo, air form and/or flat iron the hair straight before sculpting. By straightening the hair first, you will see how long the hair actually is and be able to sculpt accordingly.

If the hair will be worn naturally curly, you may first wish to shampoo and towel-dry the hair. Drying the hair thoroughly will allow you to observe the natural curl formation. After observing the hair in its natural state, spray the hair with water to lightly moisten it. Sculpting the hair while damp rather than wet reduces the amount of stretching. **Sculpting hair partly wet and partly dry will result in an uneven effect.**

Consider the shrinkage factor while sculpting curly hair. Stretching or applying tension to curly hair while sculpting may result in shorter lengths than anticipated. You may choose to use a comb instead of your fingers to control curly hair while sculpting. The comb allows for minimal tension so that you can view how the hair will fall naturally.

Sculpting Dry Versus Wet Hair

Generally designers sculpt their client's hair after the shampoo while the hair is still damp. The advantages to dry sculpting include being able to see how the hair falls naturally and observing the shape of the sculpture as it is being created. Ultimately, it is a matter of preference and situation that determine whether to sculpt wet, dry or both. Keep in mind, if you cut curly hair while wet, there will be some shrinkage in length when it dries. Tool choice is another consideration: choose clippers for dry hair, a razor on damp hair, and shears on dry or wet hair.

Using the 7 Sculpting Procedures will allow you to achieve predictable results each time you create a hair sculpture for your client. Awareness of hair growth patterns, fringe, nape and curly hair considerations will allow you to personalize the form.

LESSONS LEARNED

>> The 7 Sculpting Procedures performed in sequential order are: Section, head position, part, distribute, project, finger/shear position, and design line.

1. **Section** – Sectioning divides the hair into workable areas for control

2. **Head Position** – Head position directly influences the fall of the hair; includes upright, forward and tilted

3. **Part** – Partings subdivide sections of hair to separate, distribute and control the hair while sculpting; includes horizontal, vertical and diagonal

4. **Distribute** – Direction hair is combed in relation to the base parting; includes natural, perpendicular, shifted and directional

5. **Project** – Angle at which hair is held prior to sculpting, includes common angles of 0°, 45° and 90°

6. **Finger/Shear Position** – Position of the fingers and shears relative to the base parting; includes parallel and nonparallel

7. **Design Line** – Artistic pattern or length guide used while sculpting any straight or curved line from the celestial axis, which can be stationary or mobile

>> The additional factors to consider while sculpting hair:

- Growth Patterns – Widows peak, cowlick and whorl

- Fringe and Nape Variations – Adapted to client's face and neck shape

- Curly Hair Considerations – Based on how hair will be worn naturally; may be sculpted dry or wet

105ᶜ.4 // SCULPTURE
GUEST EXPERIENCE

EXPLORE //

What types of things influence whether you become a regular client at a salon or a spa?

≫ INSPIRE //

Providing an exceptional guest experience will ensure that clients return to you for future sculpture services.

ACHIEVE //

Following this lesson on *Sculpture Guest Experience*, you'll be able to:

>> Summarize the service essentials related to hair sculpture

>> Provide examples of how to reassure or calm a child during a sculpting service

>> Provide examples of infection control and safety guidelines for sculpture services

FOCUS //

SCULPTURE GUEST EXPERIENCE

Sculpture Service Essentials

Children as Clients

Sculpture Infection Control and Safety

105ᶜ.4 | SCULPTURE GUEST EXPERIENCE

The guest experience begins with building rapport and trust with your client. Communicating with your client prior to, and during the service will help you avoid misunderstandings and ensure predictable results. Pay close attention to all the cues the client may be giving you. Use photos and magazines while talking with your client to clarify design intentions.

≫ SCULPTURE SERVICE ESSENTIALS

To make a memorable impression on your client, pay attention to the following guidelines when performing the hair sculpture service–from the initial greeting to the completion of the service.

CONNECT

≫ Meet and greet the client with a firm handshake and a pleasant tone of voice.

≫ Communicate to build rapport and develop a relationship with the client.

CONSULT

≫ Ask questions to discover client wants and needs. Questions such as, "Did you have a specific reason for selecting this particular haircut?" and "What do you like, or dislike, about your previous haircut?" will help bring out what the client really wants, and areas of concern the client might have.

≫ Ask questions about their lifestyle, such as "How much time do you have to spend on your hair?" If the client is leading a hectic lifestyle, you probably won't want to suggest a high-maintenance haircut.

≫ Ask questions about other services the client may desire, such as coloring or relaxing their hair. Keep in mind that each service can complement another, and as a designer, you will need to consider how the cut will affect the color design and vice versa. Explain the cost and maintenance associated with both services.

≫ Ask specific questions such as, "Would you like layers in your hair?" or "Would you like your ears or your neck exposed?" to uncover client expectations for their hair design.

≫ Analyze your client's face and body shape, physical features, hair and scalp.

≫ Assess the facts and thoroughly think through your recommendations by visualizing the end result.

≫ Explain your recommended solutions, products, and the price for today's service(s) as well as for future services.

≫ Gain feedback from your client and obtain consent before proceeding with the service.

Refer to lessons on the four Service Essentials, *Design Connection* and *Client Considerations* for further guidelines.

Refer to the lesson on
*Shampoo and Scalp Massage
Theory* for further guidelines.

CREATE

>> Ensure your client is protected by draping them with a towel and plastic cape during the shampoo process.

>> Perform a scalp massage to relax the client while shampooing their hair.

>> Replace the towel with a neck strip for the actual sculpting procedures.

>> Ensure client comfort during the service.

>> Stay focused on delivering the sculpture service to the best of your ability.

>> Explain to your client the products you are using throughout the service, and why.

>> Allow the client to hold the product and to test it in their palm to become familiar with the scent and feel.

>> Produce a functional, predictable and pleasing result.

>> Personalize the hair sculpture, which may include texturizing techniques, after you air form the hair to add your signature touch.

>> Remove any stray hairs from the client's face and clothing.

>> Teach the client how to perform at-home hair care maintenance.

COMPLETE

>> Request specific feedback from your client. Ask questions and look for verbal and nonverbal cues to determine your client's level of satisfaction.

>> Escort client to the retail area and show the products you used. Products may include shampoo and conditioner or styling and finishing products. Recommend products to maintain the appearance and condition of your client's hair.

>> Invite your client to make a retail purchase for home care.

>> Prebook – Suggest a future appointment time for your client's next visit.

>> Offer sincere appreciation to your client for visiting the school or salon.

>> Complete client record for future visits; include recommended products.

CHILDREN AS CLIENTS

Although many children pose no challenge when performing a haircut, some children do need to be treated more carefully to help alleviate their fears and concerns. You can offer reassurance to a timid child or calm down a boisterous one by taking a few simple steps prior to and during a professional hair service.

>> In the reception area, kneel down and make eye contact with the child or sit down next to them.

>> Introduce yourself and, if the child is very young, explain what is about to take place. Use fun language when explaining the process. For example, talk about the "ride" in the chair when you pump it up and the cape that they can wear, just like superheroes.

>> If the parent and child allow you, take a young child by the hand as you lead him or her to your workstation.

>> While performing the service, maintain continual eye and voice contact. Keep the child informed of everything you are doing. Use firm, but not rough or jerky motions as you work with the child's head and hair to instill confidence.

>> Keep in mind that many young children do not know the difference between left and right. You might try putting different colored hair clips on their shoelaces and refer to them when you need the child to move their head in a certain direction.

>> To keep a child from squirming, offer a reward, such as a balloon, if they cooperate. You can also remind the child that squirming may cause you to cut yourself. Do not, however, tell a child that you might cut them.

>> If an older child or teenager comes into the salon without a parent and requests a haircut, consider calling the parent first to gain permission. Ask your salon manager for the salon's policy regarding unaccompanied minors.

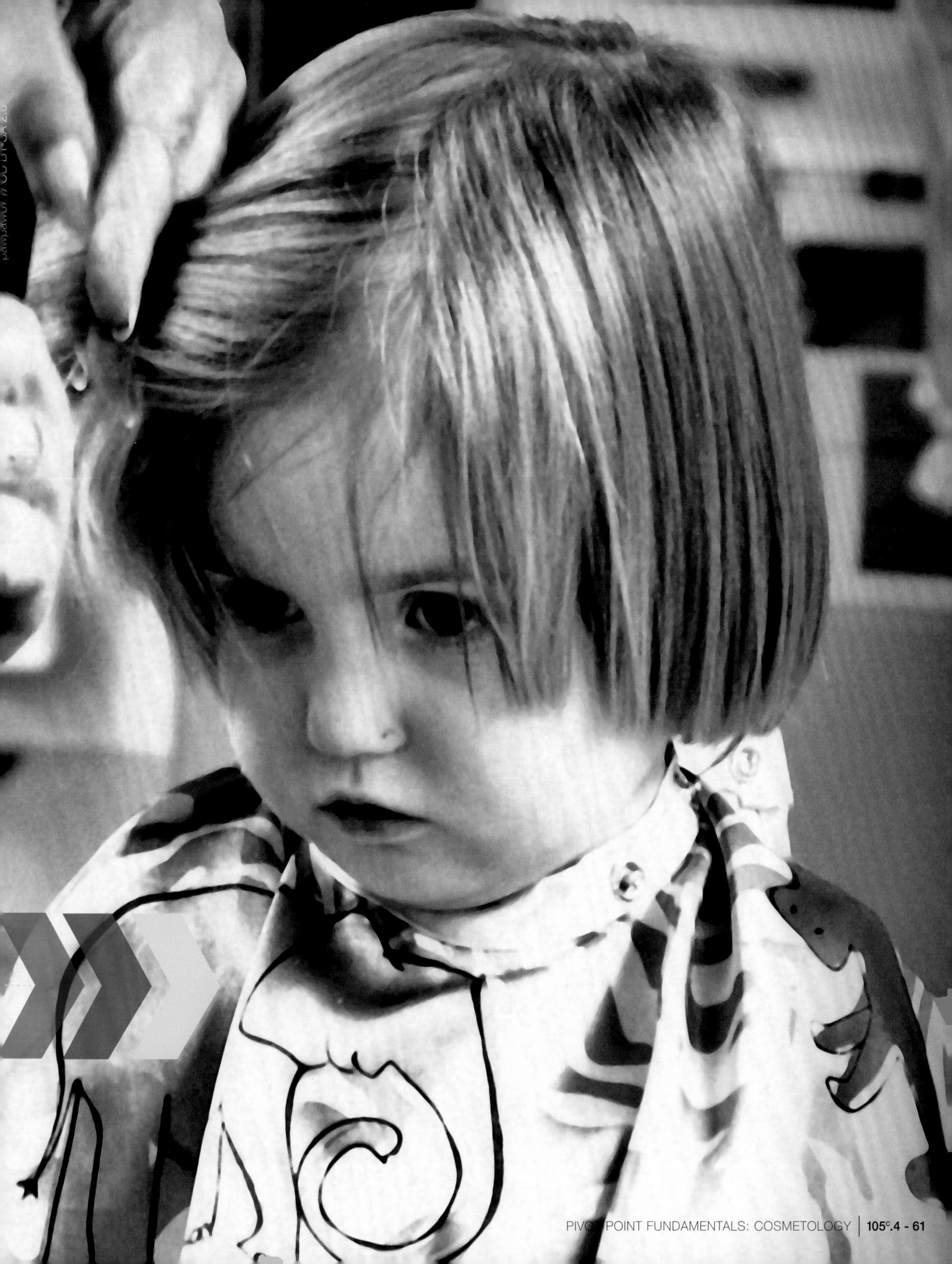

COMMUNICATION GUIDELINES

Following are a few cues that you might hear from a client during the consultation, and suggestions for responding in a way that encourages client trust and open communication.

CLIENT CUE	DESIGNER RESPONSE
"I always wanted a one-length haircut."	"Do you mean you want your hair the same length throughout, like 3" at the top, sides and back? Or, do you mean that you want your hair to fall to the same area on your body, like your jawline, neck or shoulders? If you mean the same area, I have the perfect diagonal-forward haircut in mind for you. It will emphasize your jawline. This cut will be shorter in the back, and longer toward your face. It's not all 'one length,' but I think you'll love the movement it creates."
"I just want a trim."	"How much do you think you want trimmed? Would you like a half-inch, an inch, or more? I don't want to cut your hair too short."
"I only want three layers."	"Are you saying you only want some layering at the bottom? Or, would you like three very distinct lengths at the bottom? And do you want your layers to blend?" "Please show me where you would like your shortest layer to start. I can blend the layers from the shortest layer to the longest length at the perimeter to avoid a 'choppy' look, or if you prefer, I can create three distinct levels in your hair."
"I want layers, but not too many."	"Where exactly would you like the layers? Would you like layers that frame your face only? I think soft layers around your face will accent your features and give you plenty of styling options. Or, if you prefer layers only at the top, that will give you added volume."
"I don't like the shape of my haircut, and I can't do anything with these curls."	"I can re-shape your hair to give you expansion at the sides and back to emphasize your cheeks and expose your neckline. I think shifting the weight upward will also give you a more youthful appearance. I also have some recommendations for a shampoo, leave-in conditioner and styling products you can use at home to enhance your natural curl pattern."
"Last time I had my hair cut, it was texturized so much that now I feel like I'm bald."	"I'm sorry you had that bad experience. Texturizing hair can be tricky. With your hair texture, I know exactly what type of texturizing techniques to use to give your hair added volume and mobility. However, I don't have to texturize your hair today; we can wait until you feel more comfortable. And once you do, I will be happy to explain exactly what I'm doing, and why."
"My hair is too round. I prefer a more masculine look at the sides and top, and also at the neckline."	"I can definitely do that for you. A square form usually has a weight corner where the sides and top meet. Many times, this area is cut off, making it round. I'll create a straight line vertically from your ear to the hairline, and I'll cut a horizontal line across your nape. This will give you a more masculine nape line."

SCULPTURE INFECTION CONTROL AND SAFETY

It is your responsibility as a professional to protect your client by following infection control and safety guidelines with any and all services you provide.

Cleaning is a process of removing dirt, debris and potential pathogens to aid in slowing the growth of pathogens. Cleaning is performed prior to disinfection procedures.

Disinfection methods kill certain pathogens (bacteria, viruses and fungi) with the exception of spores. Disinfectants are available in varied forms, including concentrate, liquid, spray or wipes that are approved EPA-registered disinfectants available for use in the salon industry. Immersion, and the use of disinfecting spray or wipes are common practices when it comes to disinfecting tools, multi-use supplies and equipment in the salon. Be sure to follow the manufacturer's directions for mixing disinfecting solutions and contact time, if applicable.

CLEANING AND DISINFECTION GUIDELINES

Keep in mind that only nonporous tools, supplies and equipment can be disinfected. All single-use items must be discarded after each use. Always follow your area's regulatory guidelines.

TOOLS, SUPPLIES AND EQUIPMENT	CLEANING GUIDELINES	DISINFECTION GUIDELINES
Shears/Taper Shears	» Remove hair and debris. » Open hinged area to allow for thorough cleaning. » Preclean with soap and water.	» Use an approved EPA-registered disinfectant solution, wipe or spray.
Razor	» Discard disposable razor blades after each use in a puncture-proof container. » Open hinged area to allow for thorough cleaning. » Preclean with soap and water.	» Use an approved EPA-registered disinfectant solution, wipe or spray. » Immerse razor (without blade) in disinfectant solution.
Clippers and Trimmers	» Remove guards. » Remove hair and debris. » Preclean guard with soap and water.	» Use an approved EPA-registered disinfectant solution or spray. » Be guided by clipper manufacturer's directions for disinfecting.
Combs and Brushes	» Remove hair and debris. » Preclean with soap and water.	» Immerse in an approved EPA-registered disinfectant solution.
Cape (plastic and cloth)	» Remove hair from cape. » Wash in washing machine with soap after each use.	» Some regulatory agencies may require use of an approved EPA-registered disinfectant.
Neck Strip	» Single-use item; must be discarded.	» Cannot be disinfected.

Store disinfected tools and multi-use supplies in a clean, dry, covered container or cabinet.

If tools, multi-use supplies or equipment have come in contact with blood or body fluids, the following disinfection procedures must take place:

 Use an approved EPA-registered hospital disinfectant according to manufacturer's directions and as required by your area's regulatory agency.

CARE AND SAFETY

Follow infection control procedures for personal care and client safety guidelines before and during the sculpture service to ensure your safety and the client's, while also contributing to the salon care.

Personal Care		Client Care Prior to the Service	
	» Clean and disinfect tools appropriately.		» Check the scalp for any diseases or disorders. If any are evident, refer the client to a physician and do not proceed with the service.
» Check that your personal standards of health and hygiene minimize the spread of infection.	» Wear single-use gloves as required.	» Protect the client's skin and clothing from water with a freshly laundered towel and a freshly laundered plastic or waterproof cape.	» Handle cutting tools with care to ensure your safety and that of your clients.
» Wash hands and dry thoroughly with a single-use towel.	» Refer to your area's regulatory agency for proper mixing/handling of disinfectant solutions.	» Protect the client's skin and clothing from cut hair by replacing the towel with a neck strip following the shampoo service.	» If any tools are dropped on the floor be sure to pick them up, then clean and disinfect.
» Disinfect workstation.	» Minimize fatigue by maintaining good posture during the service.	» Be sure the cape stays in place and the client's arms are underneath the cape.	» Complete the client record noting scalp/hair condition.

Client Care During the Service

>> Work carefully around nonremovable jewelry/piercings.

>> If you cut the client or yourself, stop service immediately and apply first-aid procedures.
  ■ If wound is deep, seek emergency medical attention.

>> Be aware of nonverbal cues the client may be conveying.

>> Remove hair clippings from client's eyes, face and neck.

>> Store soiled towels in a dry, covered receptacle until laundered.

>> Be aware of scalp sensitivity while combing client's hair.

>> Be cautious and avoid nicking moles and skin tags.

Salon Care

>> Sweep or vacuum and dispose of hair clippings prior to air forming and at the end of the service.

>> Follow health and safety guidelines, including cleaning and disinfecting guidelines.

>> Ensure electrical equipment, plugs and cables are in good condition, and remember to turn off after use.

>> Ensure equipment, including the salon chair and shampoo chair, is clean and disinfected.

>> Ensure electrical cords are properly positioned to avoid accidental falls.

>> Promote a professional image by ensuring your workstation is clean and tidy throughout the service.

>> Report malfunctioning furniture/equipment to manager.

>> Disinfect all tools after each use. Always use disinfected combs and brushes for each client.

>> Clean/mop water spillage from floor to avoid accidental falls.

DISCOVER**MORE**

Regulatory Agency – It's the Law!

It's up to you to know and follow your area's regulatory guidelines on cleaning and disinfection procedures. Legally, salons are required to protect the public, so you too must be aware of the law. Follow salon practices and when you become a salon owner, research your area's regulatory agency guidelines—most often posted online. Document your results for easy access.

SALON**CONNECTION**

To Clean and Disinfect, or to Throw Away? That Is the Question!

In the salon, s up to you to follow cleaning and disinfection procedures. Knowing what to clean and disinfect and what to throw away is critical to ensure a safe salon environment. If it is designed for single use, use it once and discard it. If it is designed to be a multi-use supply, disinfect it. Stay current with your area's regulatory agency to prevent the spread of diseases.

By following the four Service Essentials, making adjustments for children who are clients, and following proper infection control and safety guidelines, you will be able to create a pleasant salon experience and build a loyal clientele.

LESSONS LEARNED

The service essentials related to hair sculpture can be summarized as follows:

- Connect – Meet and greet client to build rapport.

- Consult – Ask questions to discover client needs; analyze clients face, body shape, physical features, hair and scalp; assess the facts to make recommendations; explain recommended solutions and gain feedback for consent to move forward.

- Create – Ensure client safety and comfort; stay focused to deliver the best service; teach and explain the products to your client; teach the client at-home care maintenance.

- Complete – Request specific feedback; recommend the products you used; suggest future appointment times; complete client record.

>> Ways to reassure or calm a child during a sculpture service include kneeling down and making eye contact, using fun language to explain the service and offering a reward such as a balloon.

>> Infection control and safety guidelines must be followed throughout a sculpture service to ensure your safety and the safety of the clients and the salon. Disinfectants are available in varied forms, including concentrate, liquid, spray or wipes that have EPA approval for use in the salon industry. Be guided by your area's regulatory agency for proper cleaning and disinfection guidelines.

105ᶜ.5 //

SCULPTURE SERVICE

EXPLORE //

Can you think of a time you made a haircut appointment and felt like you didn't get the "full treatment"?

INSPIRE //

Before, during and after—paying attention to details ensures a loyal client base!

ACHIEVE //

Following this lesson on *Sculpture Service*, you'll be able to:

>> Provide examples of guidelines to ensure client comfort and satisfaction when performing a sculpture service

>> Describe the three areas of a sculpture service

FOCUS //

SCULPTURE SERVICE

Sculpture Client Guidelines

Sculpture Service Overview

Sculpture Rubric

105°.5 | SCULPTURE SERVICE

This lesson is a culmination of everything you have learned about sculpture theory, tools, skills and guest relations; it's where you apply your knowledge, before, during and after the hair sculpture service to ensure client comfort and satisfaction.

SCULPTURE CLIENT GUIDELINES

To ensure your client's comfort and satisfaction during the sculpture service, keep the following guidelines in mind when performing the sculpture procedure.

SECTION

>> Consider natural growth patterns and hair density.

>> Use light pressure when positioning sectioning clips to avoid scratching client's scalp.

>> Avoid over-twisting hair and clip section in direction of parting to avoid tangling hair.

>> Clip hair away from face to ensure client can see comfortably.

HEAD POSITION

>> Choose a head position that allows you to judge projection as well as angles of partings and finger position while sculpting.

>> Explain to clients why it is important they maintain same head position in order to achieve accurate results.

>> Move head slowly and gently when changing from one head position to another to ensure client safety and comfort.

PART

>> Avoid pulling hair by combing section into direction it will be parted prior to taking parting.

>> Use wide-toothed side of sculpting comb to part hair gently.

DISTRIBUTE

›› Use fine teeth of comb to distribute hair.

›› Use wide teeth of comb to avoid pulling hair for thicker hair density or curly texture.

PROJECT

›› Ensure client's head is in proper position when measuring or determining projection angle.

›› Measure projection angle from natural fall or curve of head.

FINGER/SHEAR POSITION

›› Avoid applying excessive tension while holding hair with fingers.

›› Avoid wearing rings that may get caught in client's hair.

›› Groom fingernails frequently to avoid scratching client or hair getting caught in broken or torn nails.

›› Palm the shears to avoid cutting client or yourself.

DESIGN LINE

›› Establish length guide for design line in natural fall first to ensure lengths are not shorter than desired.

›› Keep partings thin so design line is visible.

SCULPTURE SERVICE OVERVIEW

The Sculpture Service Overview identifies the three areas of all sculpture services:

>> The Sculpture Preparation provides a brief overview of the steps to follow *before* you actually begin the hair sculpture.

>> The Sculpture Procedure provides an overview of the 7 Sculpting Procedures that you will use *during* the hair sculpture to ensure predictable results.

>> The Sculpture Completion provides an overview of the steps to follow *after* performing the hair sculpture to ensure guest satisfaction.

SERVICE ESSENTIALS: THE FOUR Cs

The Sculpture Procedure includes attention to the four Cs.

1. **Connect**
   Establishes rapport and builds credibility with each client

2. **Consult**
   Analyzes client wants and needs, visualizes the end result, organizes the plan for follow-through and obtains client agreement

3. **Create**
   Produces functional, predictable and pleasing results

4. **Complete**
   Reviews the service experience and client satisfaction, offers product recommendations, expresses appreciation and provides follow-up

SCULPTURE SERVICE OVERVIEW

SCULPTURE PREPARATION	» Clean and disinfect workstation. » Arrange disinfected sculpting tools and supplies including shears, razor with guards and disposable blades, combs, sectioning clips and spray bottle. » Wash your hands. » Perform analysis of hair and scalp. » Ask client to remove jewelry; store in secure place.
SCULPTURE PROCEDURE	» Drape client for a wet service. » Shampoo and condition client's hair. » Replace client's towel with neck strip. » Perform 7 Sculpting Procedures to achieve desired results: 1. **Section** hair into workable areas for purpose of control. 2. **Position head** as either upright, tilted or forward. 3. **Part** to separate, distribute and control hair (horizontal, vertical, diagonal). 4. **Distribute** hair (natural, perpendicular, shifted, directional). 5. **Project** hair appropriately for desired structure (natural fall, 0°, 45°, or 90°, low, medium, high). 6. **Position fingers/shears** (parallel and/or nonparallel). 7. Sculpt appropriate **design line** (horizontal, vertical, diagonal, and stationary or mobile). » Texturize the sculpted form as appropriate (base, midstrand and/or ends). » Cross-check for accuracy. » Perform finishing design procedures to include personalizing form.
SCULPTURE COMPLETION	» Reinforce client's satisfaction with overall salon experience. » Make professional product recommendations. » Prebook client's next appointment. » End guest's visit with warm and personal goodbye. » Discard single-use supplies, disinfect tools and multi-use supplies, disinfect workstation and arrange in proper order. » Sweep or vacuum hair clippings from floor to prevent slipping. » Wash hands. » Complete client record.

SCULPTURE RUBRIC

A performance rubric is a document that identifies defined criteria at which levels of performance can be measured objectively. The following rubric is an example that your instructor might choose to use for scoring. The Sculpture Rubric is divided into three main areas—Preparation, Procedure and Completion. Each area is further divided into step-by-step procedures that will ensure client safety and satisfaction.

SCULPTURE RUBRIC

Allotted Time: 45 Minutes

Student Name:_____ ID Number: _____

Instructor: _____ Date: _____ Start Time: _____ End Time: _____

SCULPTURE (Live Model) – *Each scoring item is marked with either a "Yes" or "No." Each "Yes" counts for one point. Total number of points attainable is 34.*

CRITERIA	YES	NO	INSTRUCTOR ASSESSMENT
PREPARATION: *Did student...*			
1. Set up workstation with properly labeled supplies?	☐	☐	
2. Place disinfected tools and supplies at a visibly clean workstation?	☐	☐	
3. Wash their hands?	☐	☐	
Connect: Did student...			
4. Meet and greet client with a welcoming smile and pleasant tone of voice?	☐	☐	
5. Communicate to build rapport and develop a relationship with client?	☐	☐	
6. Refer to client by name throughout service?	☐	☐	
Consult: Did student...			
7. Ask questions to discover client's wants and needs?	☐	☐	
8. Analyze client's hair and scalp and check for any contraindications?	☐	☐	
9. Gain feedback and consent from client before proceeding?	☐	☐	
PROCEDURE: *Did student...*			
10. Properly drape client and prepare for service?	☐	☐	
11. Ensure client protection and comfort by maintaining cape on outside of chair at all times?	☐	☐	
12. Carry out appropriate shampoo and condition procedures?	☐	☐	
13. Use products economically?	☐	☐	
Create: Did student...			
14. Section hair for control?	☐	☐	
15. Position client's head in accordance with sculpture?	☐	☐	
16. Part hair using appropriate and consistent partings?	☐	☐	
17. Distribute hair accurately from partings?	☐	☐	
18. Project hair from partings to achieve desired result?	☐	☐	
19. Position fingers/shears accurately while sculpting?	☐	☐	
20. Sculpt appropriate design line(s)?	☐	☐	
21. Cross-check sculpture for balance and accuracy?	☐	☐	
22. Teach client to use products to maintain appearance and condition of their hair?	☐	☐	
23. Remove hair clippings from skin and cape?	☐	☐	
24. Practice infection control procedures and safety guidelines throughout service?	☐	☐	
COMPLETION *(Complete)*: *Did student...*			
25. Ask questions and look for verbal and nonverbal cues to determine client's level of satisfaction?	☐	☐	
26. Make professional product recommendations?	☐	☐	
27. Ask client to make a future appointment?	☐	☐	
28. End guest's visit with a warm and personal goodbye?	☐	☐	
29. Discard single-use supplies?	☐	☐	
30. Disinfect tools and multi-use supplies, disinfect workstation and arrange in proper order?	☐	☐	
31. Sweep or vacuum hair clippings from floor completely?	☐	☐	
32. Complete service within scheduled time?	☐	☐	
33. Complete client record?	☐	☐	
34. Wash their hands following service?	☐	☐	

COMMENTS: _____ TOTAL POINTS = _____ ÷ 34 = _____ %

SALON**CONNECTION**

It's All in the Details!
In the salon, you may be pressed for time, however it's important to follow all the steps necessary to ensure client satisfaction. Omitting steps from the sculpture service can mean the difference between a satisfied or not-so-satisfied client.

DISCOVER**MORE**

Practice Makes Permanent!
What makes top-performing athletes champions? World-class champion soccer player and coach Bobby Robson has a saying: "Practice makes permanent"—a great reminder on the importance of practice. What you practice will become second nature!

Applying all aspects of a sculpture procedure each and every time you perform a hair sculpture service will help you ensure client safety and satisfaction.

LESSONS LEARNED

Sculpture client guidelines to follow to ensure comfort and satisfaction include:

>> Considering client's natural growth patterns and hair density before sectioning the hair

>> Positioning the client's head to accurately judge projection angles

>> Using the wide teeth of the comb to part the hair

>> Distributing the hair in the direction the hair will be parted

>> Measuring projection angles from natural fall or from the curves of the head

>> Grooming fingernails to avoid scratching client

>> Keeping partings thin so the stationary/mobile design line remains visible at all times

The three areas of a sculpture service include Preparation, Procedure and Completion:

>> Preparation includes greeting the client, arranging workstation and performing a hair and scalp analysis.

>> Procedure includes following the 7 Sculpting Procedures and texturizing the hair to personalize the form.

>> Completion includes reinforcing client's satisfaction, making product recommendations, rebooking next appointment and disinfecting workstation.

EXPLORE //

Which historical or contemporary figure do you think popularized the "bob"?

INSPIRE //

Classic, yet timeless, the solid form can be adapted to set trends.

ACHIEVE //

Following this *Solid Form Overview,* you'll be able to:

>> Identify the characteristics of solid form
>> Provide examples of the 7 Sculpting Procedures related to the solid form
>> Give examples of guidelines to follow when sculpting solid form
>> Provide fringe design variations that can be incorporated into solid form sculptures

FOCUS //

SOLID FORM OVERVIEW

Solid Form Characteristics
Solid Form Sculpting Procedures
Solid Form Guidelines

105°.6 | SOLID FORM OVERVIEW

The solid form is one of the most requested haircuts offered in the salon due to its versatility. The characteristics of a pure solid form include:

>> Maximum weight at the perimeter

>> Unactivated texture with unbroken lines

>> Lengths falling to the same level

SALON**CONNECTION**

More Than One Way to Say It!
In the salon, a client might refer to the solid form as a blunt cut, one-length cut, or bob. In other instances, they might describe the overall look or feel of the cut, such as a smooth surface with blunt ends.

It is up to you to stay current with the type of terminology that a client might use to describe a desired look. Search the Internet to learn about trendy solid form haircuts such as the "lob."

SOLID FORM CHARACTERISTICS

Part of making appropriate design decisions is becoming familiar with the characteristics of the solid form, which include the shape—rectangular; texture—unactivated; and structure—shorter exterior lengths progressing to longer interior lengths.

SHAPE

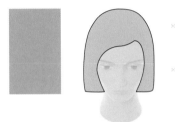

» Analyzing the shape of solid form hair sculptures will reveal similarities that are most evident on straight hair.

» Near the top, the shape echoes the curves of the head. At the bottom, an angular form line is a result of the weight buildup at the perimeter, resulting in an overall rectangular shape.

» Permed or natural curl texture will expand the shape's dimension, particularly at the perimeter weight area.

» Solid form hair sculptures can be created along various lines and at many different lengths.

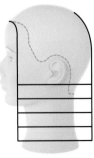

HORIZONTAL

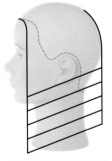

DIAGONAL FORWARD

DIAGONAL BACK

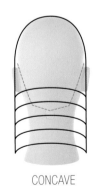

CONCAVE

CONVEX

TEXTURE

Solid form on straight hair:

>> The texture of the solid form is unactivated with smooth, unbroken lines on the surface.

>> The longer lengths from the interior fall over the rest of the hair in the exterior and reach the perimeter of the design.

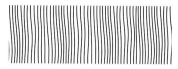

Solid form on wavy or curly hair:

>> Surface appears activated, even though the lines are unbroken.

>> The activation is a result of the curl pattern, not the sculpted form.

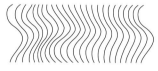

>> With tighter curl patterns, solid form lengths may appear layered.

STRUCTURE

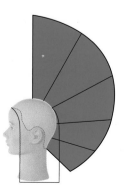

>> Solid form lengths progress from shorter at the exterior to longer in the interior.

>> In natural fall, all lengths fall to one level, creating weight at the perimeter form line.

>> Color-coded blue.

SOLID FORM SCULPTING PROCEDURES

Understanding and mastering how the 7 Sculpting Procedures are used to achieve solid form lengths will allow you to create predictable results.

SECTION (1)

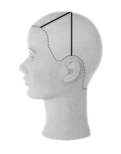

- » Section for control
- » Section between design line changes
- » Sectioning may include a center or off-center parting

HEAD POSITION (2)

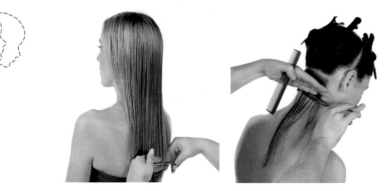

- » When sculpting solid form, the head is generally held in an upright position.
- » When refining the nape hairline, the head may be tilted forward.

PART (3)

» The parting pattern for solid form is generally parallel to the design line. Common parting patterns include:

HORIZONTAL DIAGONAL FORWARD DIAGONAL BACK CONCAVE CONVEX

DISTRIBUTE (4)

Natural distribution is the most common type of distribution used to sculpt solid forms.

Natural distribution takes growth patterns into account:

» Pay particular attention to the area above the crest.

» Place minimal tension on the hair.

» Allow hair to fall naturally over the curve of the head.

» Solid fringes require natural distribution around the front hairline to create a precise line.

» Freeform, or free-hand sculpting is often used to sculpt the fringe area. Freeform sculpting is cutting the hair without holding or controlling the lengths with your fingers or comb. With freeform sculpting, the eyes and hands are the only means of control.

Before sculpting a solid form without fringes:

» Comb the front lengths in the direction they will be worn to ensure that the hair will fall to one level in the finished design.

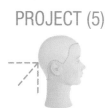

PROJECT (5)

The two projection angles used to sculpt solid forms are:

» Natural fall

» Zero degrees (0°)

NATURAL FALL

» When the hair is in natural fall, it is neither lifted away from the scalp nor moved toward it.

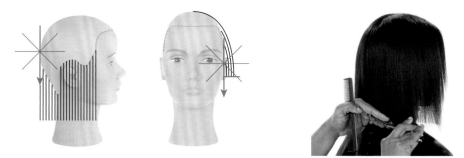

0° PROJECTION

» 0° positions the hair flat against the surface of the head.

» In some areas of the head, natural fall and 0° may be the same.

To refine a solid form line, sculpt on the skin at 0°.

To increase the underbeveled effect:

» Tilt the head forward.

» Sculpt at 0° projection.

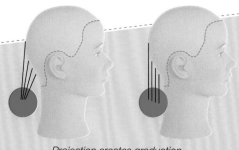

Projection creates graduation

The most important thing to remember about projection for solid forms is to maintain natural fall or 0° projection and avoid lifting the hair, which creates graduation.

FINGER/SHEAR POSITION (6)

To sculpt the solid form, most often fingers and shears are positioned parallel to the part and the desired form line.

Alternate methods of controlling the hair can be used to create a solid form.

| PALM UP | PALM DOWN | BACK OF HAND | COMB CONTROL |

>> The sculpting hand may be turned with the palm up or the palm down.

>> The method used depends on the level of comfort relative to the length of the hair and the line being sculpted, as well as the area of the head being sculpted.

>> The back of your hand or a comb can be used to control the hair.

>> With comb control, the angle of the comb establishes a guide to follow.

DESIGN LINE (7)

» A stationary design line is used to sculpt solid forms.

» The direction of the design line establishes the perimeter form line.

» Once the stationary design line is established all subsequent partings are distributed to the stationary design line.

HORIZONTAL

DIAGONAL FORWARD

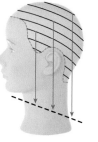

DIAGONAL BACK

CONCAVE

CONVEX

SOLID FORM GUIDELINES
TENSION

» Whether sculpting on straight or curly hair, too much tension will result in a graduated appearance.

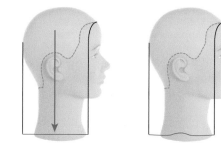

» Avoid tension when sculpting over the ears.

» Variations in the hairline and the protrusion of the ears can cause uneven lengths if too much tension is applied.

» To avoid tension around the ear, use the back of the comb, your finger or your closed shears to compress the hair slightly toward the head before sculpting. The resulting slack will allow for the shape and protrusion of the ear.

Comb Control

» Comb control can be used to sculpt solid form with the least amount of tension.

» The comb is placed parallel to the design line, and the shears are positioned parallel to the comb.

Freeform

» Another way to avoid tension when sculpting solid forms is to use freeform sculpting techniques.

Curly Hair

» Note how much longer curly hair appears when tension is used.

» To maintain the shape of the solid form, you may use an overlapping technique. This is done by sculpting each parting slightly longer as you work up the head.

» The form line is then refined by sculpting with the tips of the shears if needed.

» Sometimes it is preferable to sculpt curly hair after it has been air formed straight, referred to as dry sculpting. Dry sculpting allows you to observe the shape or form as it is being sculpted.

LONGER LENGTHS

» Often, the design decisions you make with your client will include lengths well below the shoulders.

» Since solid forms require sculpting a precise line, you may need to make slight adjustments in your technique.

» Turning the client's head to one side and then to the other to sculpt the sides is helpful.

» You may then sculpt either in front or in back of the shoulders.

» When turning the head, keep the position of the chin consistent from one side to the other to maintain the line that you are sculpting.

» To create a horizontal line with a slight increase toward the sides, shift the hair toward the back.

» This allows you to sculpt on the flatter surface of the back.

SOLID FORM FRINGE VARIATIONS

Solid form designs may be customized with the addition of a solid fringe or different types of fringes. All fringe designs should be personalized to adapt to the features of your client's face as well as growth patterns and hair density in the fringe area. Here are a few examples:

 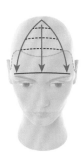

>> A solid fringe can frame the eyes.

>> Length and design can vary.

>> A layered fringe adds texture and mobility.

>> Texturizing techniques can add more end texture.

>> A longer fringe offers various styling options.

>> The concavity of the fringe can be symmetrical or asymmetrical, depending on the part.

DISCOVER**MORE**

Total Composition

Solid form haircuts can range in length from short to medium to long. The surface appearance can be altered with the addition of texture, such as waves or spiral curls. Color can also be added to break up the light reflection to create the illusion of texture. Search the Internet for color pattern ideas that can enhance the solid form.

The solid form will be a style you give to many salon clients. Master the 7 Sculpting Procedures needed to create a solid form to meet all your clients' needs.

LESSONS LEARNED

» The solid form has a rectangular shape. The texture is unactivated and the structure is shorter lengths in the exterior progressing to longer lengths in the interior.

» When sculpting solid form:

1. Section – Done for control and between design line changes

2. Head Position – Generally upright

3. Part – Horizontal and diagonal

4. Distribute – Natural

5. Project – Natural fall and 0°

6. Finger/Shear Position – Parallel to the parting and desired form line

7. Design Line – Horizontal, diagonal, and both straight and curved combinations; all lengths are distributed to a stationary design line

» When sculpting solid forms avoid tension over the ear. Use comb control to sculpt with the least amount of tension. A freeform sculpting technique can be used to avoid tension. When sculpting curly hair, the overlapping technique can be used, or air form the hair straight before sculpting. For longer lengths, turn the client's head to one side or the other and sculpt behind or in front of the shoulder.

» With the solid form, a solid fringe can frame the eyes. A layered fringe adds texture and mobility, while a longer fringe offers various styling options.

SOLID FORM
HORIZONTAL LINE

EXPLORE

Have you ever had a difficult time creating something that you thought looked so simple?

INSPIRE

Hair designers need to be able to sculpt the solid form along a horizontal line since it is a basic and classic hair sculpture that can be adapted to meet current trends.

ACHIEVE

Following this *Solid Form, Horizontal Line Workshop*, you'll be able to:

>> Identify the 7 Sculpting Procedures related to the solid form, horizontal line

>> Sculpt a balanced solid form along a horizontal line using natural distribution and no projection

>> Create fullness and a curved-under effect by air forming the solid form using a 9-row brush

This sculpture exhibits a smooth, totally unactivated surface with the focus on the horizontal line and perimeter weight.

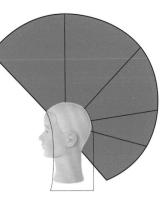

Shorter exterior lengths progress to longer interior lengths.

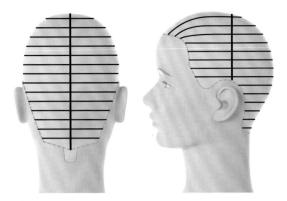

Use consistent horizontal partings throughout and maintain a parallel finger/shear position.

7 SCULPTING PROCEDURES

1. SECTION:
   (4) Center front hairline to nape; ear to ear

2. HEAD POSITION: Upright

3. PART: Horizontal

4. DISTRIBUTE: Natural

5. PROJECT: Natural fall

6. FINGER/SHEAR POSITION: Parallel

7. DESIGN LINE: Horizontal; stationary

DESIGN DECISIONS CHART

SOLID FORM HORIZONTAL LINE

Draw or fill in the boxes with the appropriate answers.

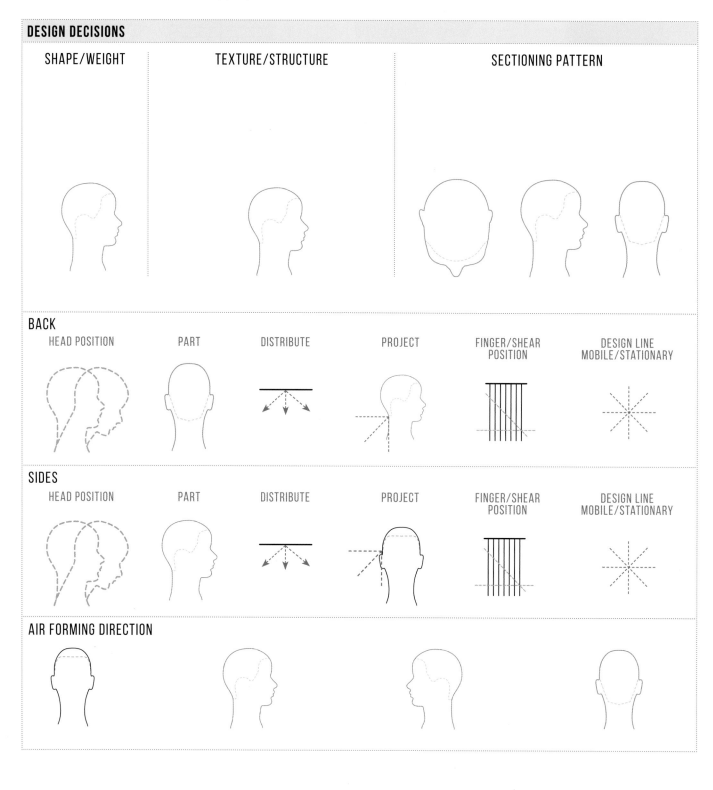

DESIGN DECISIONS

SHAPE/WEIGHT	TEXTURE/STRUCTURE	SECTIONING PATTERN

BACK

HEAD POSITION	PART	DISTRIBUTE	PROJECT	FINGER/SHEAR POSITION	DESIGN LINE MOBILE/STATIONARY

SIDES

HEAD POSITION	PART	DISTRIBUTE	PROJECT	FINGER/SHEAR POSITION	DESIGN LINE MOBILE/STATIONARY

AIR FORMING DIRECTION

Instructor Signature _____ Date _____

PERFORMANCE GUIDE

SOLID FORM HORIZONTAL LINE

View the video, complete the Design Decisions chart, then perform this workshop. Complete the self-check as you progress through the workshop.

40 mins
Suggested Salon Speed

PREPARATION		✔
	» Assemble tools and products » Set up workstation	☐

SECTIONING AND HEAD POSITION		
	1. Section hair into 4 areas: » Forehead to nape » Apex to each ear	☐

DESIGN LINE – NAPE		
	2. Position head upright.	☐
	3. Sculpt design line from center to one side, then from center to opposite side: » Horizontal parting » Natural distribution » No projection » Parallel finger/shear position » Stationary horizontal design line	☐
	4. Check the design line for balance before continuing.	☐
	5. Sculpt nape: » Horizontal partings (subdivide for control) » Natural distribution » No projection » Parallel finger/shear position » Stationary horizontal design line *Alternate sculpting from the center to one side, then from the center to the opposite side.*	☐

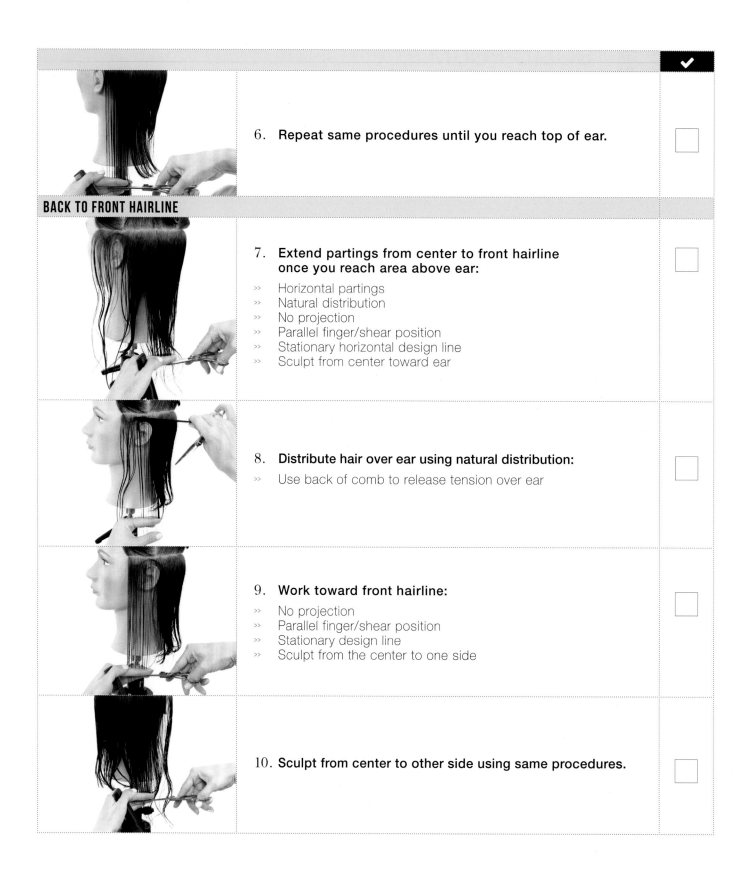

6. **Repeat same procedures until you reach top of ear.**

BACK TO FRONT HAIRLINE

7. **Extend partings from center to front hairline once you reach area above ear:**
   - » Horizontal partings
   - » Natural distribution
   - » No projection
   - » Parallel finger/shear position
   - » Stationary horizontal design line
   - » Sculpt from center toward ear

8. **Distribute hair over ear using natural distribution:**
   - » Use back of comb to release tension over ear

9. **Work toward front hairline:**
   - » No projection
   - » Parallel finger/shear position
   - » Stationary design line
   - » Sculpt from the center to one side

10. **Sculpt from center to other side using same procedures.**

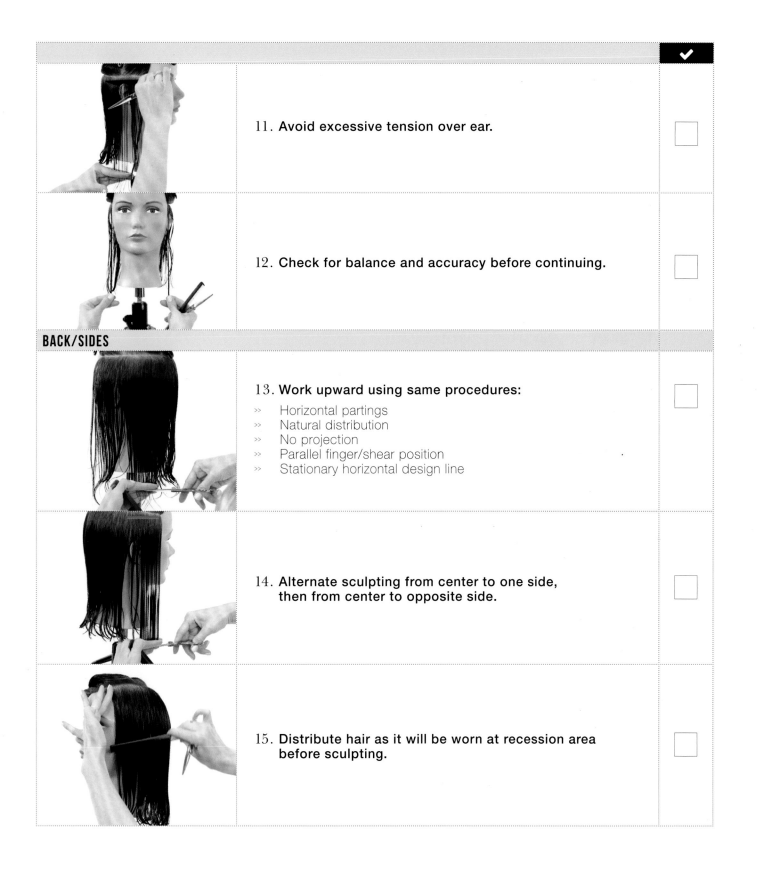

11. Avoid excessive tension over ear.

12. Check for balance and accuracy before continuing.

BACK/SIDES

13. Work upward using same procedures:
    >> Horizontal partings
    >> Natural distribution
    >> No projection
    >> Parallel finger/shear position
    >> Stationary horizontal design line

14. Alternate sculpting from center to one side, then from center to opposite side.

15. Distribute hair as it will be worn at recession area before sculpting.

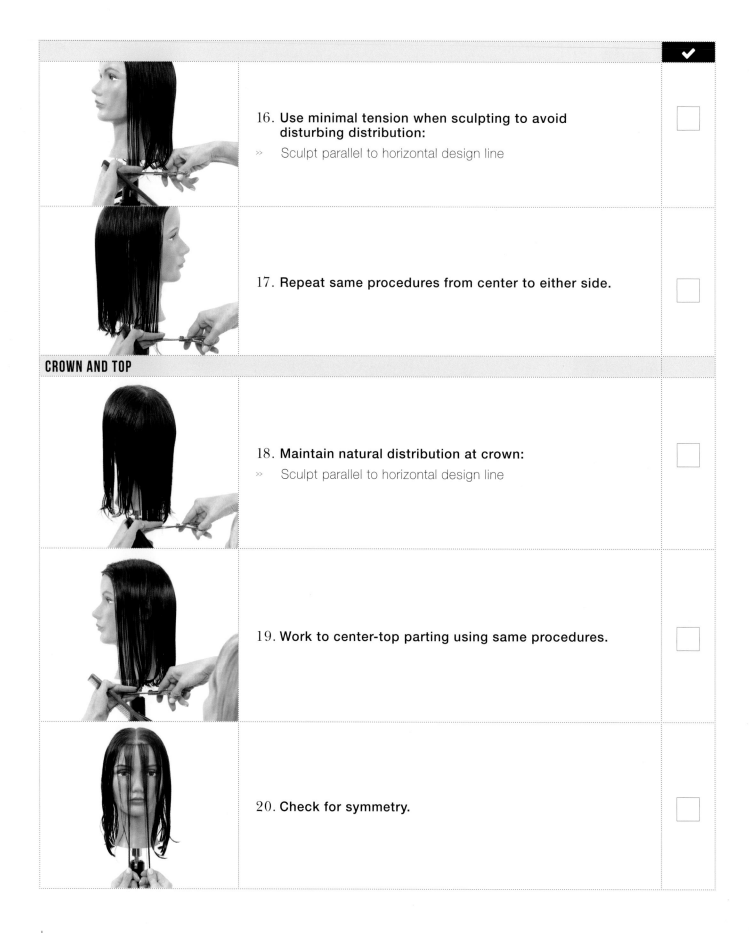

16. **Use minimal tension when sculpting to avoid disturbing distribution:**
    » Sculpt parallel to horizontal design line

17. **Repeat same procedures from center to either side.**

CROWN AND TOP

18. **Maintain natural distribution at crown:**
    » Sculpt parallel to horizontal design line

19. **Work to center-top parting using same procedures.**

20. **Check for symmetry.**

AIR FORMING 9-ROW BRUSH

21. **A horizontal parting pattern is used to air form hair.**

22. **Apply mousse throughout hair.**

23. **Use vent brush to remove moisture from hair.**

24. **Begin air forming in nape:**
    » Section hair from center front hairline to nape
    » Release horizontal parting across nape
    » Position 9-row brush parallel to horizontal parting and use only first few rows of teeth to pick up hair
    » Direct airflow with a concentrator from top as you air form base, midstrand and then ends

25. **Create a curved-under effect:**
    » Position and rotate brush under section of hair
    » Work from center to one side, and from center to other side

26. **Work upward using same procedures.**

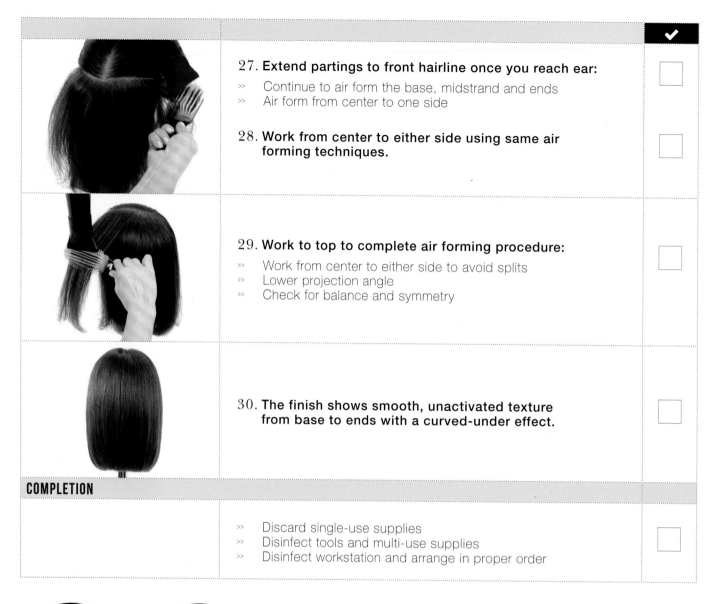

27. **Extend partings to front hairline once you reach ear:**
   >> Continue to air form the base, midstrand and ends
   >> Air form from center to one side

28. **Work from center to either side using same air forming techniques.**

29. **Work to top to complete air forming procedure:**
   >> Work from center to either side to avoid splits
   >> Lower projection angle
   >> Check for balance and symmetry

30. **The finish shows smooth, unactivated texture from base to ends with a curved-under effect.**

COMPLETION

   >> Discard single-use supplies
   >> Disinfect tools and multi-use supplies
   >> Disinfect workstation and arrange in proper order

40 mins
Suggested Salon Speed

My Speed
_____
_____
_____

INSTRUCTIONS:
Record your time in comparison with the suggested salon speed. Then, list here how you could improve your performance.

_____
_____
_____
_____

VARIATION – SOLID FORM, HORIZONTAL LINE – COMB CONTROL

A variation on the solid form, horizontal line using comb control is available online.

SOLID FORM
DIAGONAL-FORWARD LINE

EXPLORE

What do you think the greatest challenge is when sculpting diagonal lines?

INSPIRE

Diagonal lines are dynamic and imply motion as they lead the eye to a focal point.

ACHIEVE

Following this *Solid Form, Diagonal-Forward Line Workshop*, you'll be able to:

>> Identify the 7 Sculpting Procedures as related to the solid form, diagonal-forward line

>> Sculpt a balanced solid form along a diagonal-forward line using natural distribution and no projection

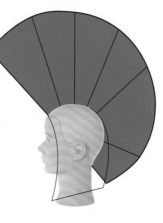

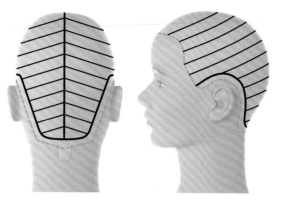

The unactivated surface texture and weight at the perimeter moves along a diagonal-forward line.

Lengths progress from shorter in the exterior to longer in the interior.

Consistent diagonal-forward partings begin in center-back and continue toward the hairline. The perimeter hairline is used to establish the length and angle of the design line.

7 SCULPTING PROCEDURES

1. SECTION:
   (2) Center front hairline to nape
   Perimeter hairline

2. HEAD POSITION: Upright

3. PART: Diagonal forward

4. DISTRIBUTE: Natural

5. PROJECT: Natural fall/0°

6. FINGER/SHEAR POSITION: Parallel

7. DESIGN LINE: Diagonal forward/Stationary

SOLID FORM DIAGONAL-FORWARD LINE

Draw or fill in the boxes with the appropriate answers.

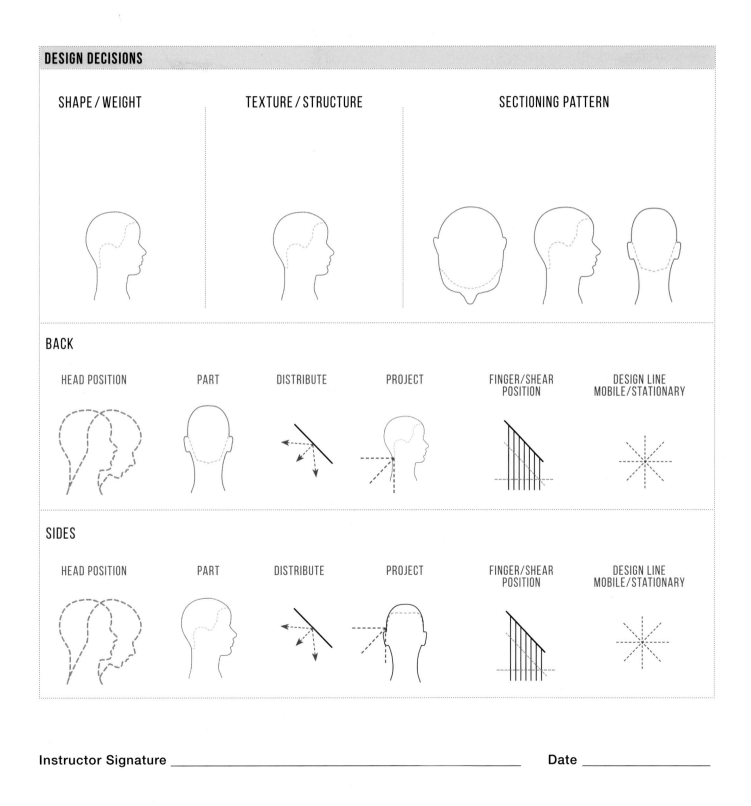

DESIGN DECISIONS

SHAPE / WEIGHT	TEXTURE / STRUCTURE	SECTIONING PATTERN

BACK

HEAD POSITION	PART	DISTRIBUTE	PROJECT	FINGER/SHEAR POSITION	DESIGN LINE MOBILE/STATIONARY

SIDES

HEAD POSITION	PART	DISTRIBUTE	PROJECT	FINGER/SHEAR POSITION	DESIGN LINE MOBILE/STATIONARY

Instructor Signature _____ **Date** _____

PERFORMANCE GUIDE

SOLID FORM DIAGONAL-FORWARD LINE

View the video, complete the Design Decisions chart, then perform
this workshop. Complete the self-check as you progress through
the workshop.

20 mins
Suggested
Salon Speed

PREPARATION	✔
>> Assemble tools and products >> Set up workstation	☐

SECTIONING – HEAD POSITION – DESIGN LINE

1. Section hair into 2 areas:

>> Front hairline to crown
>> Crown to center nape
>> Release a ½" (1.25 cm) parting along the hairline

☐

2. Position head upright. ☐

3. Determine angle of length guide: ☐

>> Angle comb from back to front

4. Sculpt design line in nape using comb control:

>> Natural distribution
>> No projection
>> Position comb diagonally
>> Stationary design line
>> Sculpt from center to one side, then other side

☐

5. Check balance and symmetry:

>> Observe line in natural fall
>> Gently pull down strands on either side to check
lengths for symmetry

☐

6. **Sculpt design line on side using comb control:**

    » Natural distribution
    » No projection
    » Position comb diagonally
    » Stationary design line
    » Sculpt from back to front hairline

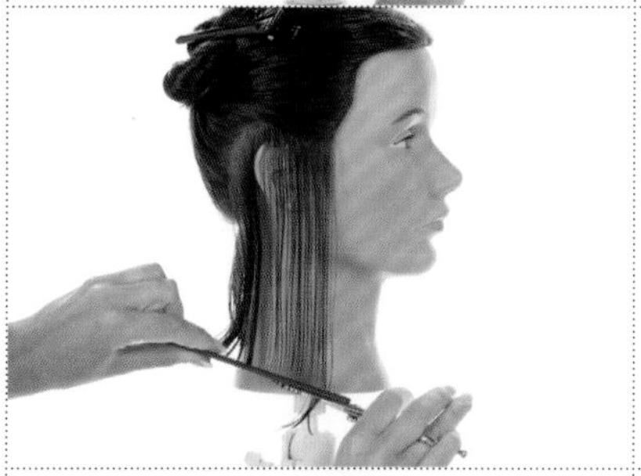

7. **Repeat same procedures on opposite side.**

8. **Check form symmetry and balance.**

LOWER BACK

9. **Sculpt lower back:**

    » Diagonal-forward partings; subdivide for control
    » Natural distribution; minimal tension
    » No projection
    » Parallel finger/shear position
    » Stationary design line

10. **Alternate from side to side using same procedures.**

11. **Check for symmetry throughout.**

BACK/SIDES | ✔

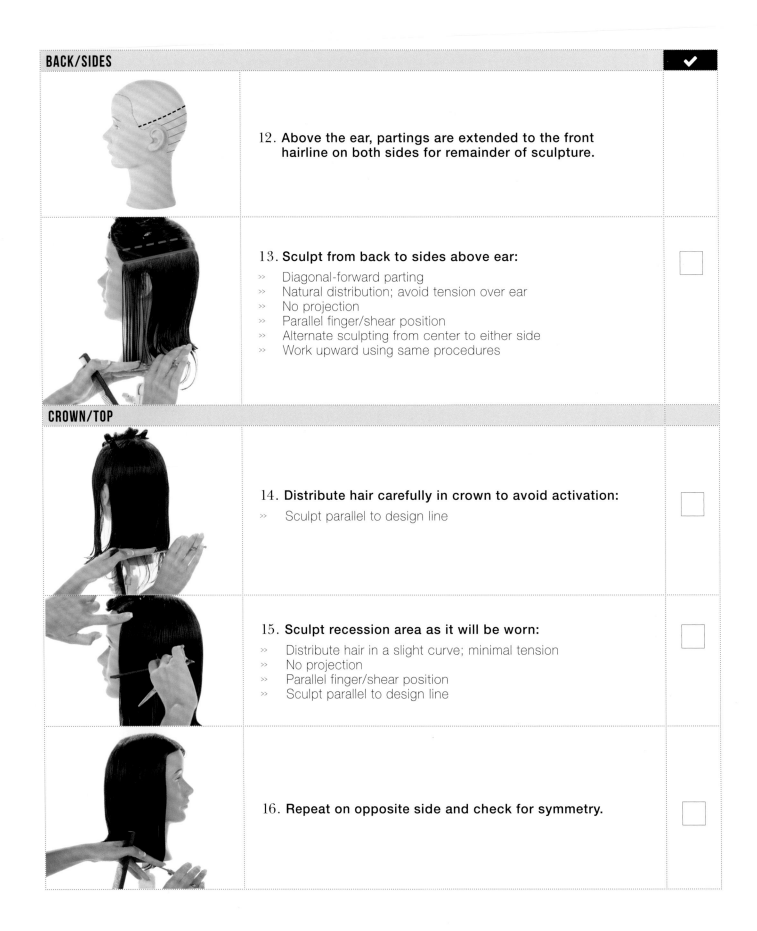

12. **Above the ear, partings are extended to the front hairline on both sides for remainder of sculpture.**

13. **Sculpt from back to sides above ear:**
    » Diagonal-forward parting
    » Natural distribution; avoid tension over ear
    » No projection
    » Parallel finger/shear position
    » Alternate sculpting from center to either side
    » Work upward using same procedures

CROWN/TOP

14. **Distribute hair carefully in crown to avoid activation:**
    » Sculpt parallel to design line

15. **Sculpt recession area as it will be worn:**
    » Distribute hair in a slight curve; minimal tension
    » No projection
    » Parallel finger/shear position
    » Sculpt parallel to design line

16. **Repeat on opposite side and check for symmetry.**

		✔
	17. Soften front corners: » Direct front lengths forward » No projection » Sculpt slightly curved line	☐
	18. Refine nape form line after air forming using comb control.	☐
	19. The finished sculpture shows a smooth surface with shorter lengths in back and longer lengths near the face, which can be styled with a center or side part.	☐

COMPLETION

	» Discard single-use supplies » Disinfect tools and multi-use supplies » Disinfect workstation and arrange in proper order	☐

20 mins
Suggested Salon Speed

My Speed
_____
_____
_____

INSTRUCTIONS

Record your time in comparison with the suggested salon speed. Then, list here how you could improve your performance.

_____

_____

_____

_____

_____

VARIATION – DRY-SCULPTING

A variation on the solid form, diagonal-forward line using a dry-sculpting technique is available online.

105^c.9 // **GRADUATED FORM OVERVIEW**

Which historical or contemporary figure do you think popularized the graduated form, also known as the "wedge"?

INSPIRE //

Triangle-shaped hair sculptures are easy to create once you master projection angles.

ACHIEVE //

Following this *Graduated Form Overview*, you'll be able to:

>> Identify the characteristics of graduated form

>> Identify the 7 Sculpting Procedures related to graduated form

>> Provide fringe design variations that can be incorporated into graduated form sculptures

FOCUS //

GRADUATED FORM OVERVIEW

Graduated Form Characteristics

Graduated Form Sculpting Procedures

Graduated Form Guidelines

105ᶜ.9 | GRADUATED FORM OVERVIEW

Graduated sculptures have grown in popularity since the 1960s. Despite the many different technical approaches that can be used to create graduated form hair sculptures, they all have a striking geometric character that features a triangular shape—the trademark of this form.

>> Smooth, unactivated interior contrasts with the activated exterior

>> Weight occurs above the perimeter form line

SALON**CONNECTION**

Listen Closely!

Graduated forms are popular in the salon. Often the graduated exterior is combined with a layered interior. You will hear clients refer to this look as a wedge, stacked bob or a modern bob. Be sure to consult with your client to know just what they are envisioning when using these terms. In many situations graduated forms are combined with other forms to create new trends.

GRADUATED FORM CHARACTERISTICS

The graduated form has a distinct shape and texture that gives the stylist countless possibilities. Graduated forms tend to be triangular in shape. The shape of the graduated form is influenced by the degree of graduation —low, medium or high.

SHAPE

LOW GRADUATION

MEDIUM GRADUATION

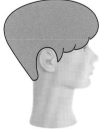

HIGH GRADUATION

With low graduation, the amount of graduated texture is minimal, resulting in the least amount of expansion.

The appearance of width is accentuated when the graduated form is sculpted on wavy or curly hair.

Shorter, high graduated forms can be combined with interior layers.

Weight

» The weight within a graduated form occurs above the perimeter form line.

» A weight line develops at the location where the longest lengths fall to rest, creating an angular corner. It is usually defined and easy to see.

» A weight area occurs at the widest angular corners of the shape where the two types of textures meet.

» Sculpting on textured hair will expand the shape and the weight area.

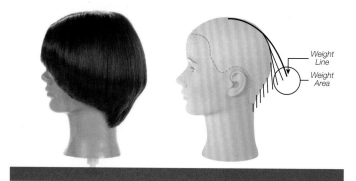

Weight Line
Weight Area

TEXTURE

» A combination of unactivated texture in the interior and activated texture in the exterior is created by the stacking of hair ends.

» The line that visually separates the two textures is called the ridge line.

» The contrasting textures are easily identified on straight hair.

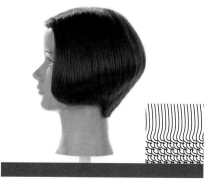

» The visual texture contrast is reduced when sculpted on wavy or curly hair.

STRUCTURE

>> Shorter exterior lengths progress toward longer interior lengths.

>> In natural fall, the ends of the hair fall close to one another and stack up along an angle.

Note how this progression varies in low, medium and high graduated forms.

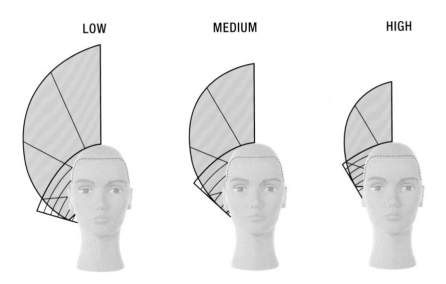

LOW   MEDIUM   HIGH

>> Color-coded yellow.

GRADUATED FORM SCULPTING PROCEDURES

Understanding and mastering the 7 Sculpting Procedures needed to achieve graduated form lengths will allow you to create predictable results.

SECTION (1)

>> Graduated forms are usually sectioned between design line or projection changes.

>> Section to subdivide large areas for control while sculpting. Depending on how the hair will be worn, sectioning may include, center front hairline to nape, or from an off-center parting to nape.

HEAD POSITION (2)

UPRIGHT

>> The head position used to sculpt graduated forms is generally upright.

TILTED FORWARD

>> The position may vary when sculpting areas such as the nape.

>> If the head position is altered, be especially careful of the distribution and projection used.

PART (3)

Any line from the celestial axis may be used. Generally the partings will be parallel to the intended form line. Common partings include:

HORIZONTAL   **DIAGONAL FORWARD**   **DIAGONAL BACK**

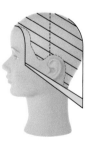

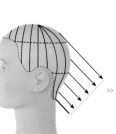

>> The exception is sculpting from vertical partings, in which case the finger position must remain diagonal to establish the line of inclination.

VERTICAL

DISTRIBUTE (4)

The most common type of distribution that is used to sculpt graduated forms is perpendicular. Natural, perpendicular and directional distribution can be used to create varying degrees of graduated texture.

NATURAL

>> Natural distribution from horizontal and diagonal partings must be combined with projection to create graduated texture.

PERPENDICULAR

>> Perpendicular distribution from diagonal partings will result in a small amount of graduation.

>> The steeper the angle of the parting the greater the amount of graduation.

>> Projection increases the amount of graduation.

DIRECTIONAL DISTRIBUTION

>> Directional distribution is used in graduated forms along vertical partings.

>> The hair is distributed diagonally downward or straight out depending on the desired degree of weight.

>> The fingers are generally positioned nonparallel along the intended line of inclination.

PROJECT (5)

>> Projection for graduated forms involves lifting the hair out of natural fall prior to sculpting.

>> It is the most commonly used method to achieve graduation.

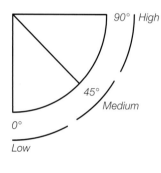

>> Lower projection angles create low graduation.

>> Higher projection angles create high graduation.

>> Low: Above 0°, below 30°

>> Medium: Above 30°, below 60°

>> High: Above 60°, below 90°

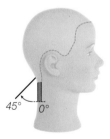

>> Often a medium (approximately 45°) angle is used as a standard.

Keep in mind that projection for graduated forms is measured from natural fall.

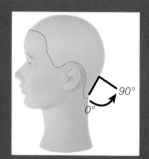

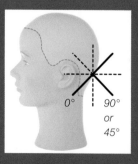

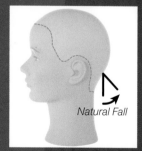

Line of Inclination

The line of inclination is the angle at which the graduation progresses in length. The first section that is projected will determine the progression of lengths.

» At the beginning of the sculpture, the line of inclination is an imaginary line that guides you in the development of the form.

» This line creates the angular silhouette that the graduated form reveals as it is being sculpted.

» All subsequent sections travel to this line, and exposed hair ends stack up along the angle of this line.

» Visualize the celestial axis to maintain consistent projection when directing the hair to the desired line of inclination.

LOW PROJECTION

» Low projection results in a low line of inclination.

» More weight is maintained in the form with a small amount of activation.

MEDIUM PROJECTION

» Medium projection results in a medium line of inclination.

» The amount of activation increases and expansion occurs with a defined weight area.

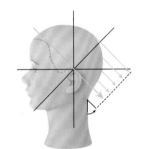

HIGH PROJECTION

» High projection results in a high line of inclination.

» The amount of activation and expansion is greater with the higher degree of projection.

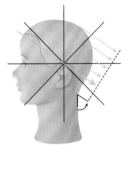

PROJECTION COMBINATIONS

Low, medium and high projection angles can all be combined within a single hair sculpture, if varying degrees of graduation are desired.

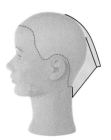

If the projection angle is lowered, the line of inclination drops and the amount of weight increases.

If the projection angle is raised, more activation and expansion in the interior of the form are created.

FINGER/SHEAR POSITION (6)

>> When sculpting graduation from horizontal and diagonal partings, in most instances your finger/shear position will be parallel to your partings.

>> The sculpting position generally positions your hands palm-to-palm.

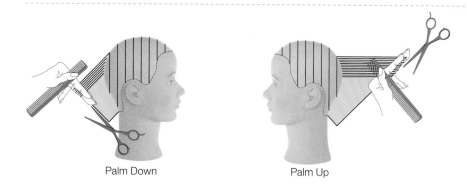

Palm Down   Palm Up

>> Graduation can also be created by using a vertical parting pattern. When sculpting graduation from vertical partings, your fingers will be positioned nonparallel to the vertical parting to establish the line of inclination.

>> Depending on the length of the hair and the area of the head, you may position your hand palm down or palm up.

DESIGN LINE (7)

Any line from the celestial axis may be used to sculpt graduation. The design line may be stationary, mobile or a combination of the two, depending on the amount of weight desired in a given area.

STATIONARY

>> For a weightier, low graduation, all lengths are projected to the first projected parting, which serves as a stationary design line.

MOBILE

>> When each section is projected consistently along the line of inclination, a mobile design line is used.

>> The previously sculpted parting is used as a length guide for the subsequent parting to be sculpted.

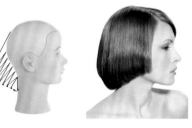

COMBINATION OF TWO

>> A combination of mobile and stationary design lines may be used.

>> A stationary design line is used when a concentration of length or a weight area is desired.

DISCOVER**MORE**

Texture and Color

Graduated form sculptures can range in length from short, to medium, to long and can be designed for ladies, men and children. When sculpted on curly hair, the visual texture contrast is reduced. When color is added, the visual contrast in textures can be exaggerated. Search the Internet for ladies and men graduated designs that include texture and color. Share your favorites with your classmates.

GRADUATED FORM GUIDELINES

CROSS-CHECKING

>> Vertical partings are often used to cross-check graduated forms.

>> The hair is parted vertically and directed out from the head.

>> The fingers are aligned with the line of inclination.

SOFTENING THE WEIGHT AREA

It is often desirable to soften the weight area of a graduated form.

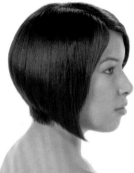

>> The hair is projected straight out from vertical partings and the weight corner is removed.

>> A notching technique can be used to remove the weight, or to texturize the hair.

>> Taper shears or a razor may be used to remove the desired amount of weight.

PRESSURE GRADUATION

>> Graduation can also be achieved by placing tension, or pressure, on wet hair, producing shorter lengths when the hair is dry.

>> Pressure graduation is especially effective on wavy or curly textures.

>> The amount of activation and expansion is greatly influenced by the degree of curl texture in the hair.

>> Assess curl pattern prior to shampooing and adjust tension for looser or tighter curl patterns while sculpting.

>> The hair may be controlled between the fingers, or it may be held flat to the head with the back of the hand or the spine of the comb.

GRADUATED FORM FRINGE VARIATIONS

A variety of fringes can alter the overall appearance of the graduated form.

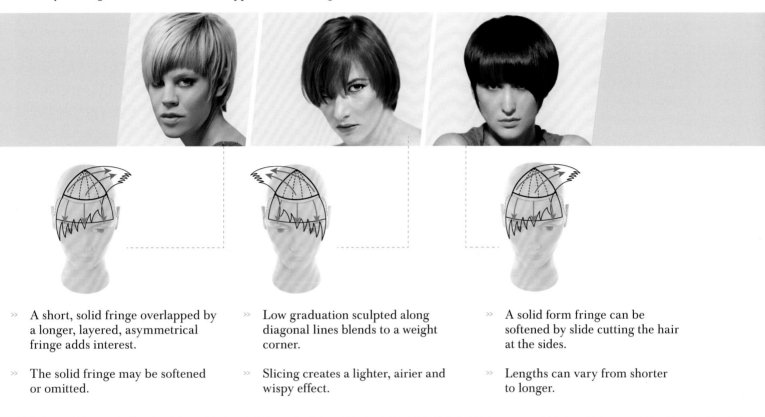

>> A short, solid fringe overlapped by a longer, layered, asymmetrical fringe adds interest.

>> The solid fringe may be softened or omitted.

>> Low graduation sculpted along diagonal lines blends to a weight corner.

>> Slicing creates a lighter, airier and wispy effect.

>> A solid form fringe can be softened by slide cutting the hair at the sides.

>> Lengths can vary from shorter to longer.

Graduated forms will likely remain a popular haircut in the salon. Understanding the graduated form characteristics, sculpting procedures and fringe design variations will enable you to personalize designs for your client.

LESSONS LEARNED

The shape of the graduated form is triangular. The unactivated texture in the interior contrasts with the activated texture in the exterior. The structure progresses in length from shorter in the exterior to longer in the interior, and in natural fall the ends of the hair fall close to one another and stack up along an angle.

>> The sculpting procedures for graduated forms include:

1. Section – Between design line or projection changes

2. Head Position – Generally upright

3. Part – Any parting from celestial axis; parallel to the intended form line

4. Distribute – Perpendicular; natural must be combined with projection; directional from vertical partings

5. Project – Low: 0° - 30°; Medium: 30° - 60°; High: 60° - 90°

6. Finger/Shear Position – A parallel finger/shear position is used from horizontal or diagonal partings, while a nonparallel finger position is used from vertical partings

7. Design Line – Any line from the celestial axis may be used to sculpt graduation; a stationary design line is used to build weight, while a mobile design line is used to create the line of inclination and the stacked effect

>> Fringes for graduated forms can range from layered asymmetrical designs to wispy effects achieved through slicing and slide-cutting techniques.

GRADUATED FORM
DIAGONAL-FORWARD LINE

EXPLORE

Have you ever worn this haircut or know someone who has? What did you like and/or dislike about it?

INSPIRE

Many clients prefer the ease of shorter hairstyles but also like the feeling of some length. This sculpture creates closeness in the nape while maintaining longer lengths toward the front.

ACHIEVE

Following this *Graduated Form, Diagonal-Forward Line Workshop*, you'll be able to:

» Identify the 7 Sculpting Procedures related to the graduated form, diagonal-forward line

» Sculpt a graduated form with a diagonal-forward line using perpendicular distribution and 30° projection

» Create fullness and a curved-under effect by air forming the diagonal-forward graduated sculpture using a 9-row brush

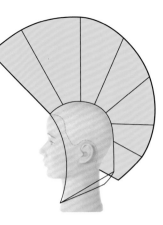
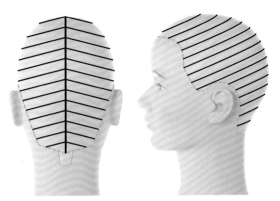

Lengths stack upon one another as activated and unactivated textures meet to create weight above the diagonal-forward perimeter form line.

Lengths progress from shorter in the exterior to longer in the interior.

Consistent diagonal-forward partings begin in center and continue toward the hairline.

7 SCULPTING PROCEDURES

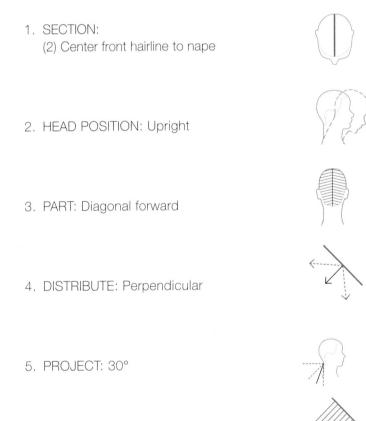

1. SECTION:
   (2) Center front hairline to nape

2. HEAD POSITION: Upright

3. PART: Diagonal forward

4. DISTRIBUTE: Perpendicular

5. PROJECT: 30°

6. FINGER/SHEAR POSITION: Parallel

7. DESIGN LINE:
   Diagonal forward; mobile/stationary

DESIGN DECISIONS CHART

GRADUATED FORM DIAGONAL-FORWARD LINE

Draw or fill in the boxes with the appropriate answers.

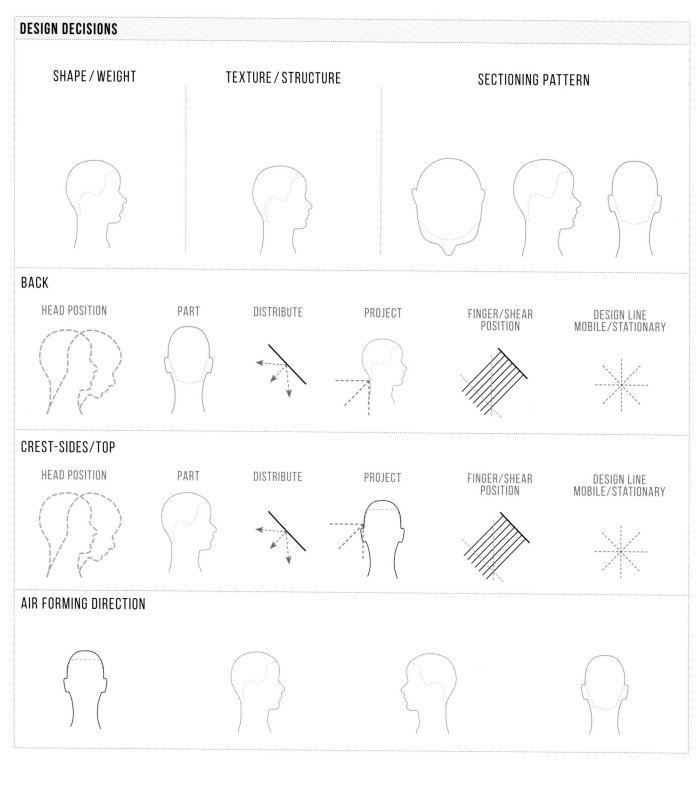

DESIGN DECISIONS

SHAPE / WEIGHT   TEXTURE / STRUCTURE   SECTIONING PATTERN

BACK

HEAD POSITION   PART   DISTRIBUTE   PROJECT   FINGER/SHEAR POSITION   DESIGN LINE MOBILE/STATIONARY

CREST-SIDES/TOP

HEAD POSITION   PART   DISTRIBUTE   PROJECT   FINGER/SHEAR POSITION   DESIGN LINE MOBILE/STATIONARY

AIR FORMING DIRECTION

Instructor Signature _____ **Date** _____

GRADUATED FORM
DIAGONAL-FORWARD LINE

View the video, complete the Design Decisions chart, then perform this workshop. Complete the self-check as you progress through the workshop.

45 mins
Suggested Salon Speed

PREPARATION	✔
>> Assemble tools and products: >> Setup workstation	☐

SECTIONING – HEAD POSITION – DESIGN LINE

1. Section hair into 2 areas: >> Front hairline to crown; crown to nape	☐
2. Position head upright.	☐
3. Part hair at a 30° diagonal-forward angle on either side of nape, resulting in a concave parting.	☐
4. Sculpt design line: >> Perpendicular distribution >> 0° projection >> Parallel finger/shear position >> Sculpt from center to one side to begin mobile design line	☐
5. Repeat on other side to complete mobile design line.	☐

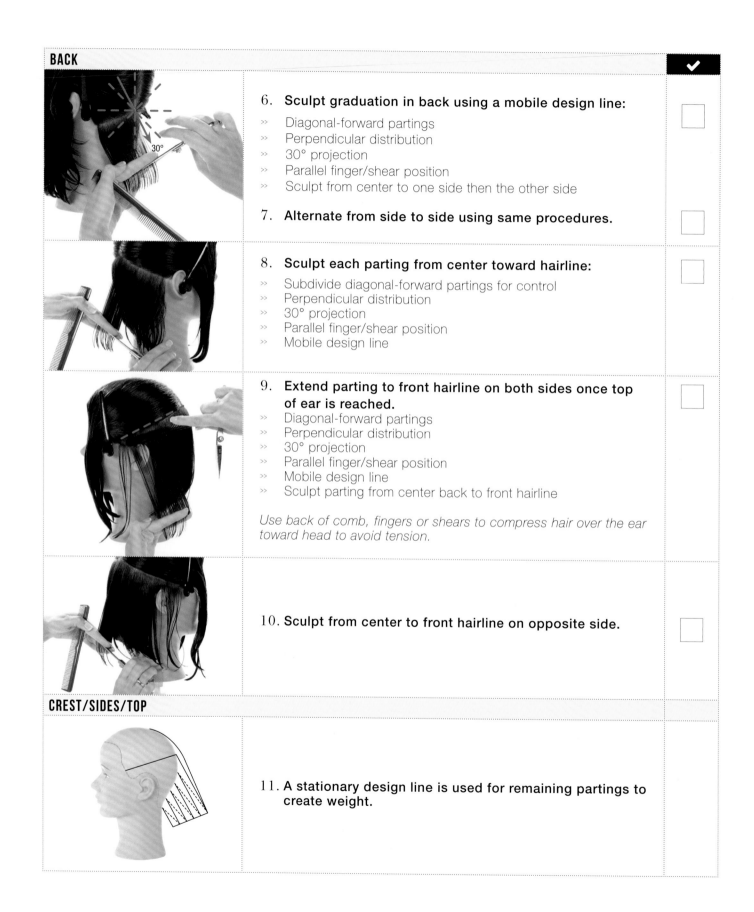

BACK ✓

6. **Sculpt graduation in back using a mobile design line:**
   - » Diagonal-forward partings
   - » Perpendicular distribution
   - » 30° projection
   - » Parallel finger/shear position
   - » Sculpt from center to one side then the other side

7. **Alternate from side to side using same procedures.**

8. **Sculpt each parting from center toward hairline:**
   - » Subdivide diagonal-forward partings for control
   - » Perpendicular distribution
   - » 30° projection
   - » Parallel finger/shear position
   - » Mobile design line

9. **Extend parting to front hairline on both sides once top of ear is reached.**
   - » Diagonal-forward partings
   - » Perpendicular distribution
   - » 30° projection
   - » Parallel finger/shear position
   - » Mobile design line
   - » Sculpt parting from center back to front hairline

   Use back of comb, fingers or shears to compress hair over the ear toward head to avoid tension.

10. **Sculpt from center to front hairline on opposite side.**

CREST/SIDES/TOP

11. **A stationary design line is used for remaining partings to create weight.**

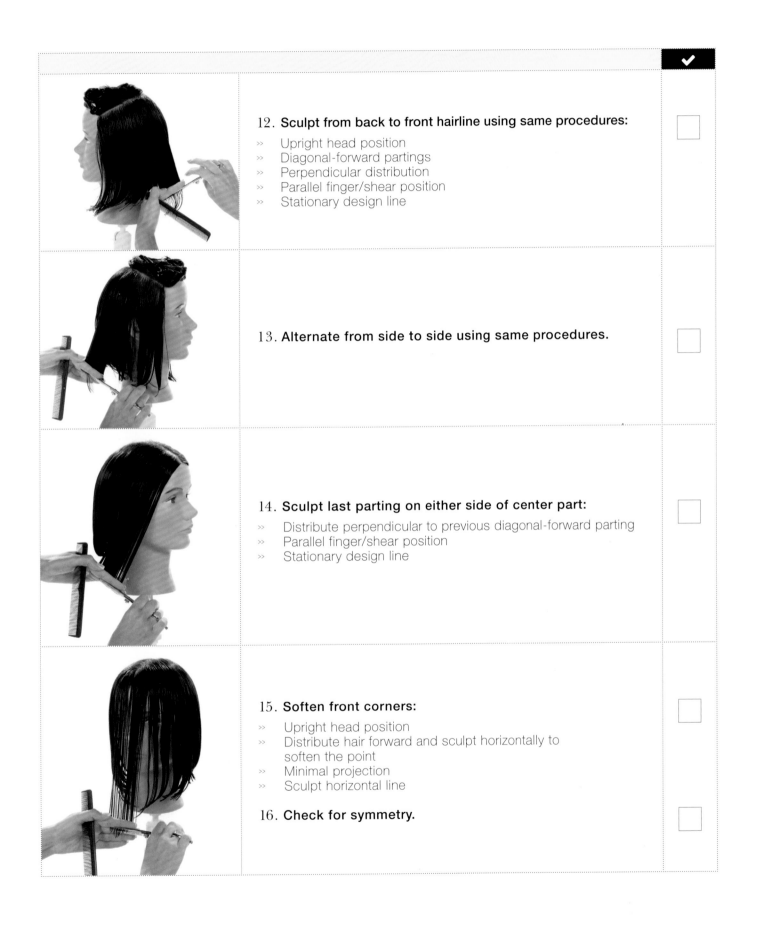

12. Sculpt from back to front hairline using same procedures:

- » Upright head position
- » Diagonal-forward partings
- » Perpendicular distribution
- » Parallel finger/shear position
- » Stationary design line

13. Alternate from side to side using same procedures.

14. Sculpt last parting on either side of center part:

- » Distribute perpendicular to previous diagonal-forward parting
- » Parallel finger/shear position
- » Stationary design line

15. Soften front corners:

- » Upright head position
- » Distribute hair forward and sculpt horizontally to soften the point
- » Minimal projection
- » Sculpt horizontal line

16. Check for symmetry.

AIR FORMING 9-ROW BRUSH

17. **Prepare hair for air forming:**
    >> Apply styling product evenly throughout hair,
       according to hair type and design preference
    >> Remove excess moisture with a vent brush and medium heat

18. **Section hair into 2 areas:**
    >> Front hairline to center nape

19. **Part hair in same manner as hair was sculpted
    in order to accentuate perimeter line.**

20. **Air form hair from base to ends using a 9-row brush:**
    >> Diagonal-forward partings
    >> Hold brush parallel to parting; curved movement
    >> Low projection
    >> Direct airflow from base to ends

21. **Air form working up head from center to either side:**
    >> Diagonal-forward partings
    >> Hold brush parallel to parting
    >> Low projection
    >> Direct airflow from base to ends

22. **Extend diagonal-forward partings to front hairline once
    you reach ear for remainder of design. Repeat same air
    forming procedures.**

23. Finish style as desired.

REFINE FORM LINE

24. **Refine perimeter and remove any unwanted hairs that may remain due to hairline irregularities or natural growth patterns:**
   » Distribute nape lengths in natural fall
   » Sculpt using tips of shears

25. **The finished sculpture shows graduated texture along diagonal-forward lines.**

COMPLETION

   » Discard single-use supplies
   » Disinfect tools and multi-use supplies
   » Disinfect workstation and arrange in proper order

45 mins
Suggested Salon Speed

My Speed
_____
_____
_____

INSTRUCTIONS:
Record your time in comparison with the suggested salon speed. Then, list here how you could improve your performance.

_____
_____
_____
_____
_____

VARIATION — GRADUATED FORM, DIAGONAL-FORWARD/HORIZONTAL LINE

A variation on the graduated form, diagonal-forward line using horizontal partings on the sides is available online.

GRADUATED FORM
DIAGONAL-BACK/CONVEX LINE

EXPLORE

Which client(s) in the salon do you think will benefit from this haircut?

INSPIRE

The diagonal-back graduated form allows clients to enjoy a short hair sculpture while retaining interior lengths for styling versatility.

ACHIEVE

Following this *Graduated Form, Diagonal-Back/Convex Line Workshop,* you'll be able to:

>> Identify the 7 Sculpting Procedures related to the graduated form, diagonal-back/convex line

>> Sculpt a diagonal-back/convex graduated form using perpendicular distribution and medium projection

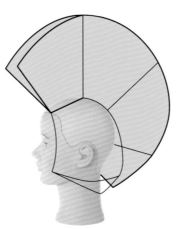
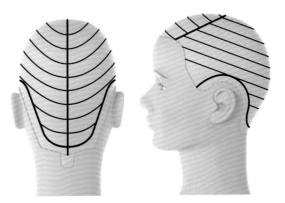

The lengths stack upon one another and create graduated texture that is sculpted along a diagonal-back line.

Lengths progress from shorter exterior to longer interior.

Consistent diagonal-back partings from a side part are slightly rounded at the center-back to avoid a point. A hairline parting is used to establish the diagonal-back design line.

7 SCULPTING PROCEDURES

1. SECTION:
   (2) Off-center part to center nape
   Perimeter hairline

2. HEAD POSITION: Upright

3. PART: Diagonal-back

4. DISTRIBUTE: Perpendicular

5. PROJECT: Medium

6. FINGER/SHEAR POSITION: Parallel

7. DESIGN LINE:
   Diagonal-back/convex; mobile

DESIGN DECISIONS CHART

GRADUATED FORM DIAGONAL-BACK/CONVEX LINE

Draw or fill in the boxes with the appropriate answers.

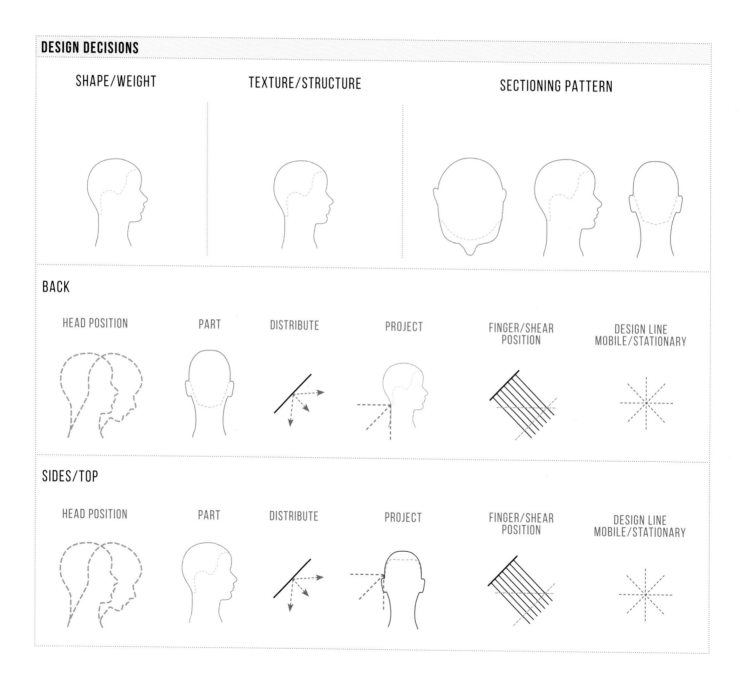

DESIGN DECISIONS

SHAPE/WEIGHT	TEXTURE/STRUCTURE	SECTIONING PATTERN

BACK

HEAD POSITION	PART	DISTRIBUTE	PROJECT	FINGER/SHEAR POSITION	DESIGN LINE MOBILE/STATIONARY

SIDES/TOP

HEAD POSITION	PART	DISTRIBUTE	PROJECT	FINGER/SHEAR POSITION	DESIGN LINE MOBILE/STATIONARY

Instructor Signature _____ **Date** _____

GRADUATED FORM
DIAGONAL-BACK/CONVEX LINE

View the video, complete the Design Decisions chart, then perform this workshop. Complete the self-check as you progress through the workshop.

20 mins
Suggested Salon Speed

PREPARATION		✔
	>> Assemble tools and products >> Set up workstation	☐

SECTIONING AND HEAD POSITION

1. **Section hair into 2 areas, from a side part:**
   >> Center of left eye to center crown
   >> Crown to center nape
   ☐

2. **Position head upright.**
   ☐

3. **Release a 1" (2.5 cm) parting along the hairline:**
   >> Front hairline to center of nape
   >> Repeat on opposite side
   ☐

DESIGN LINE

4. **Use comb to determine the angle and length of intended design line.**
   ☐

5. **Sculpt design line, beginning at front hairline on heavier side:**
   >> Upright head position
   >> Natural distribution
   >> No projection
   >> Medium-angle finger position
   >> Diagonal-back design line
   >> Sculpt parallel to fingers
   ☐

6. **Work toward center back.**
   ☐

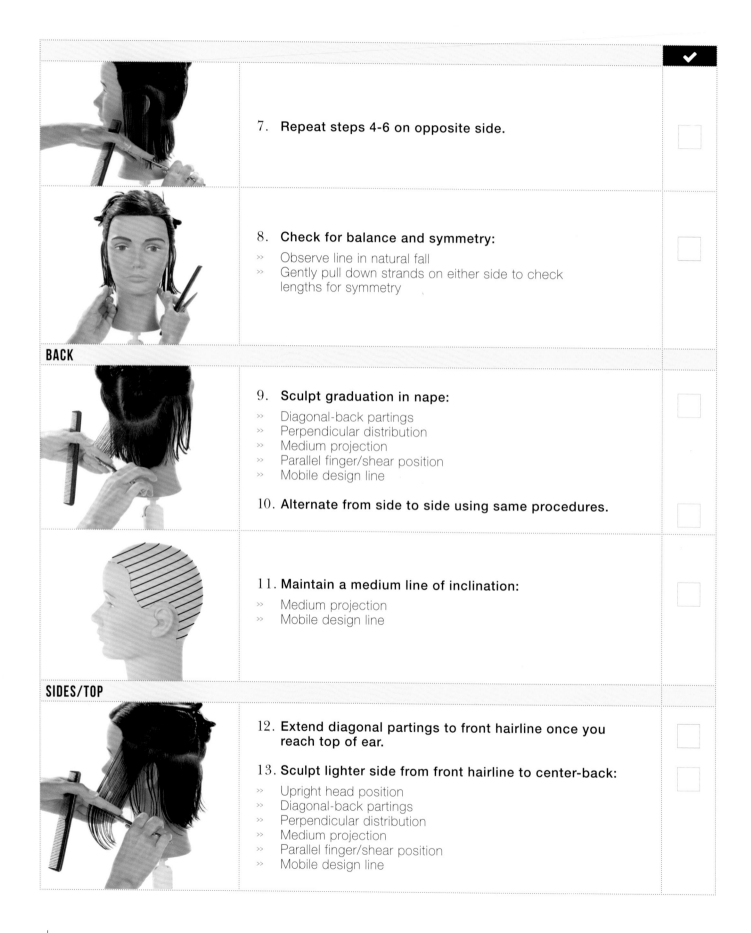

7. Repeat steps 4-6 on opposite side.

8. **Check for balance and symmetry:**
   - » Observe line in natural fall
   - » Gently pull down strands on either side to check lengths for symmetry

BACK

9. **Sculpt graduation in nape:**
   - » Diagonal-back partings
   - » Perpendicular distribution
   - » Medium projection
   - » Parallel finger/shear position
   - » Mobile design line

10. **Alternate from side to side using same procedures.**

11. **Maintain a medium line of inclination:**
    - » Medium projection
    - » Mobile design line

SIDES/TOP

12. **Extend diagonal partings to front hairline once you reach top of ear.**

13. **Sculpt lighter side from front hairline to center-back:**
    - » Upright head position
    - » Diagonal-back partings
    - » Perpendicular distribution
    - » Medium projection
    - » Parallel finger/shear position
    - » Mobile design line

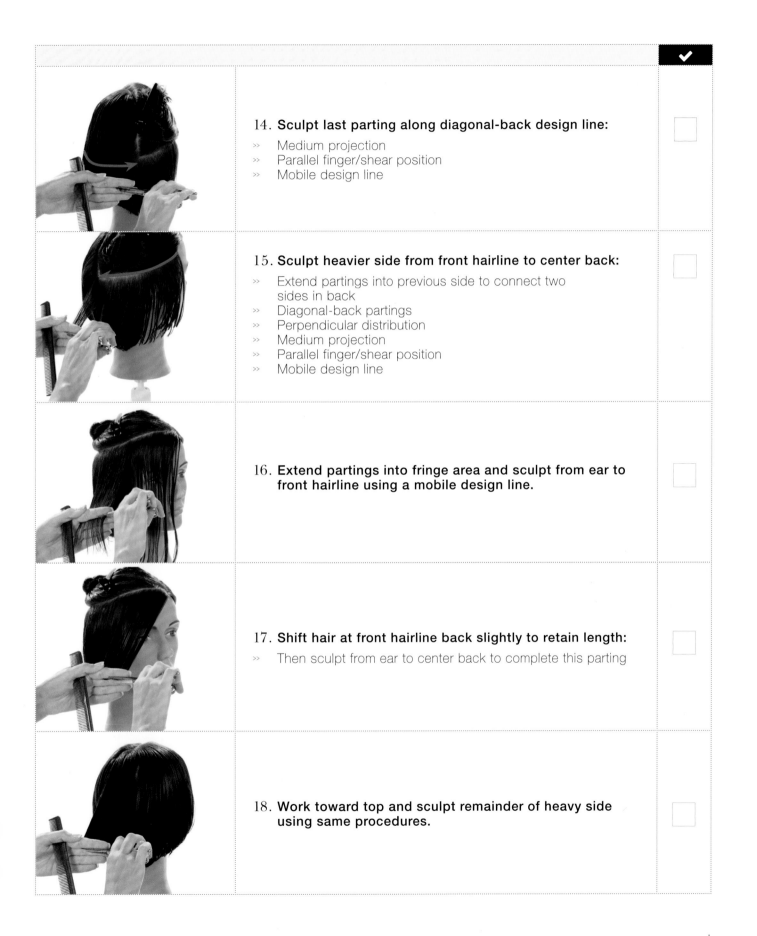

14. Sculpt last parting along diagonal-back design line:

>> Medium projection
>> Parallel finger/shear position
>> Mobile design line

15. Sculpt heavier side from front hairline to center back:

>> Extend partings into previous side to connect two sides in back
>> Diagonal-back partings
>> Perpendicular distribution
>> Medium projection
>> Parallel finger/shear position
>> Mobile design line

16. Extend partings into fringe area and sculpt from ear to front hairline using a mobile design line.

17. Shift hair at front hairline back slightly to retain length:

>> Then sculpt from ear to center back to complete this parting

18. Work toward top and sculpt remainder of heavy side using same procedures.

		✔

19. Blend/connect lighter side with heavier side:

» Distribute lengths forward
» Minimal projection
» Sculpt steep diagonal line

20. The finished sculpture shows a medium degree of graduated texture along diagonal-back lines.

COMPLETION

» Discard single-use supplies
» Disinfect tools and multi-use supplies
» Disinfect the workstation and arrange in proper order

20 mins
Suggested Salon Speed

My Speed
_____
_____
_____

INSTRUCTIONS

Record your time in comparison with the suggested salon speed. Then, list here how you could improve your performance.

_____
_____
_____
_____
_____

VARIATION — DIAGONAL-BACK LINE

A variation on the graduated form, diagonal-back line using diagonal-forward partings in the back is available online.

INCREASE-LAYERED FORM OVERVIEW

EXPLORE //

Where in nature or the arts have you seen a layered effect?

INSPIRE //

Increase layers are a popular option for long hair clients.

ACHIEVE //

Following this *Increase-Layered Form Overview*, you'll be able to:

>> Identify the characteristics of increase-layered form

>> Identify the 7 Sculpting Procedures related to increase-layered form

>> Give examples of multiple design lines used to sculpt increase-layered forms

>> Provide perimeter design options used to customize increase-layered forms

FOCUS //

INCREASE-LAYERED FORM OVERVIEW

Increase-Layered Form Characteristics

Increase-Layered Form Sculpting Procedures

Increase-Layered Form Guidelines

105°.12 | INCREASE-LAYERED FORM OVERVIEW

Increase-layered sculptures are popular and versatile and can be adapted to textures ranging from straight to wavy to curly. The surface appearance is activated with no discernible weight. Increase layers may comprise the entire form or a component of a design.

SALONCONNECTION

Keep It Long!

Many times clients come into a salon to request a new haircut, yet they don't want any perimeter length removed. Increase layers can change the shape and add volume and movement without sacrificing perimeter length. Increase-layered sculptures in the salon may also be referred to as long layers, a shag or a 180° angle cut. Search the Internet to discover increase-layered haircuts that are trendy today. Share your favorites with your classmates.

INCREASE-LAYERED FORM CHARACTERISTICS

Part of making appropriate design decisions is becoming familiar with the characteristics of the increase-layered form, which include shape (oval), texture (activated) and structure (shorter interior progressing to longer exterior).

SHAPE

>> The shape or silhouette of the increase-layered form has many variations, but in essence it is elongated, resembling an oval shape.

>> In its pure form there is no buildup of weight and no area of accentuated width.

TEXTURE

Surface Appearance

>> The texture of the increase-layered form is activated with visible hair ends that do not stack on each other.

>> When sculpting increase-layered forms, the curve of the head influences the dispersion of lengths.

>> This creates a more spread out, airier activated texture.

Long Increase

>> If the interior is sculpted at a longer length, the result is longer layers.

>> Proportionately, more of the strands will be smooth in the interior, creating a combination of unactivated textures, progressing to activated texture in the exterior.

Wavy or Curly

>> Sculpting increase-layered forms on wavy or curly hair will tend to accentuate the activated appearance of the sculpture.

>> Be aware of the length reduction that will take place as curlier textures dry.

>> Length reduction might be especially apparent on curly, shorter interior lengths.

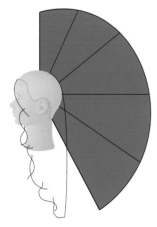

STRUCTURE

>> The length arrangement of an increase-layered form progresses from shorter interior lengths toward longer exterior lengths.

>> The shorter interior lengths create fullness, which is characteristic of the increase-layered form.

>> Color-coded red.

INCREASE-LAYERED FORM SCULPTING PROCEDURES

Understanding and mastering the 7 Sculpting Procedures needed to achieve the increase-layered form will allow you to create predictable results.

SECTION (1)

>> The hair is generally subdivided into two sections from a center or side part, depending on how the client wears their hair. The sectioning continues from the crown to the nape.

HEAD POSITION (2)

>> Head is generally positioned upright when sculpting the increase-layered form.

>> The exception is, on longer lengths, a forward head position gives you more control.

PART/DISTRIBUTE (3/4)

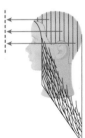

The parting pattern can be vertical, horizontal or diagonal. Generally, perpendicular distribution is used to sculpt increase-layered forms.

VERTICAL

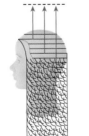

HORIZONTAL

DIAGONAL

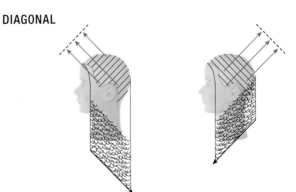

>> From vertical partings, distribute the hair forward using perpendicular distribution.

- Positions shorter lengths around the face and decreasing layered texture toward the back

>> From horizontal partings, distribute the hair upward using perpendicular distribution.

- Positions layered texture equally around the head

>> From diagonal partings, distribute the hair diagonally using perpendicular distribution.

>> Part the hair along the opposite diagonal line, then the desired perimeter form line.

- The opposite diagonal line is used when increase-layered texture is designed to parallel a diagonal perimeter form line

PROJECT (5)

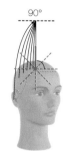

In the increase-layered form, the projection angle of the stationary design line is most important because it establishes the location to which all other lengths are converged. The farther hair travels to reach the design line, the longer the result.

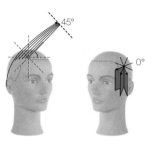

>> The projection angle of the stationary design line is usually 90°.

>> The projection angle can vary, either increasing or decreasing the distance that lengths travel to reach it.

>> To achieve a consistent projection angle, stand opposite the length increase and direct the hair toward the stationary design line.

FINGER/SHEAR POSITION (6)

The finger and/or shear position used to sculpt increase-layered forms may be parallel or nonparallel depending on the desired length increase.

PARALLEL

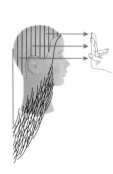

>> A parallel finger position from a horizontal parting will create even layering.

>> A parallel finger position from a vertical parting will create shorter side lengths with diagonal back layering.

NONPARALLEL

>> With a nonparallel finger position, the fingers are angled from the initial length guide (the shortest point of the sculpture) to the perimeter length.

>> A nonparallel finger position allows you to have shorter layers while conserving the perimeter lengths.

Slide Cutting

>> Another technique used to sculpt increase layering is slide cutting with the shears.

>> The shortest length is established, and the shear is closed as it glides through the hair toward the longest length.

- This is a more freeform cutting line, often curved in nature, that results is a rapid length increase. This technique is ideal for wavy or curly hair.

DESIGN LINE (7)

Any straight line from the celestial axis may be used to sculpt increase-layered forms.

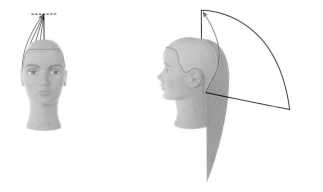

>> The most common increase-layering technique is conversion layering. This technique uses a stationary design line.

>> Once the design line is sculpted, remaining lengths are converged to this line to create a length progression that increases in the opposite direction.

Multiple Design Lines

When lengths in the exterior are not long enough to reach a single stationary design line, and full texture activation is desired, multiple design lines may be used. Since the rate of increase changes within the design, the form will tend to be less elongated.

TWO STATIONARY DESIGN LINES

>> In this example, the hair on the lower half of the head travels a reduced distance to the second design line.

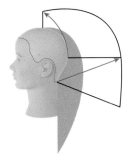

THREE STATIONARY DESIGN LINES

>> The progression of length changes according to the number of design lines used.

>> The perimeter length is affected by establishing additional design lines.

INCREASE-LAYERED FORM GUIDELINES

CUSTOMIZING THE PERIMETER DESIGN LINES

Many clients will desire perimeter weight, which is often achieved by sculpting the perimeter design line in natural fall before or after the increase-layered texture is sculpted. The amount of solid form depends on the desired result.

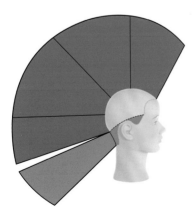

DISCOVER**MORE**

On the Fringe

Increase layering is a great technique that can be incorporated into specific areas of the design such as the nape or fringe. When a client is requesting a wispy nape or a sweeping fringe, increase-layering techniques can achieve that effect. Search the Internet to find female and male haircuts with increase-layered fringes. Share your favorites with your classmates.

If distinctly more weight and expansion are desired, you might choose to sculpt graduation in the exterior. This example shows increased layers in the interior, sculpted over a graduated exterior, resulting in expansion where the two forms meet.

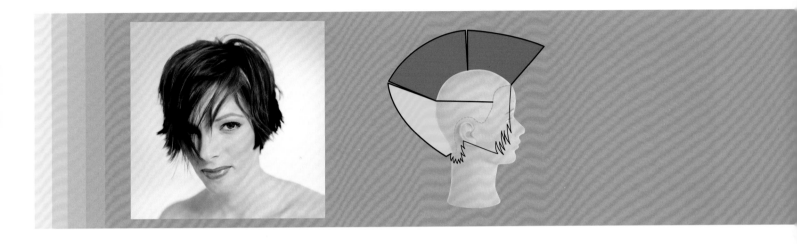

The increase-layered form is popular and versatile, allowing clients to keep length while still retaining layers that create volume, texture and directional movement.

LESSONS LEARNED

>> The characteristics of the increase-layered form are an elongated shape, resembling an oval, and an activated surface texture. The structure consists of shorter interior lengths progressing toward longer exterior lengths.

>> When sculpting increase-layered forms, sectioning is generally from a side or center part depending on how the client wears their hair. The head position is generally upright. Perpendicular distribution is used from vertical, horizontal or diagonal partings. The projection angle—0°, 45° or 90°—is established by the first parting for which all subsequent partings are converged. Finger/shear position can be either parallel or a nonparallel. A stationary design line, and the conversion-layering technique, is used to sculpt increase layers.

>> When lengths in the exterior are not long enough to reach a single stationary design line, and full texture activation is desired, multiple stationary design lines may be used.

>> The perimeter of the increase-layered form may be customized with solid or graduated forms to add weight or expansion.

INCREASE-LAYERED FORM
DIAGONAL-FORWARD LINE

EXPLORE

What options for change would you offer clients who love their long hair?

INSPIRE

Long increase-layered sculptures add volume and face-framing texture, while retaining maximum length.

ACHIEVE

Following this *Increase-Layered Form, Diagonal-Forward Line Workshop,* you'll be able to:

>> Identify the 7 Sculpting Procedures as related to the increase-layered form, diagonal-forward line

>> Sculpt a long increase-layered sculpture from diagonal-forward partings using the conversion-layering technique

>> Create a textured finish using the scrunching technique

Increase layers sculpted from diagonal-forward partings create texture and movement around the face and can be sculpted in a variety of lengths.

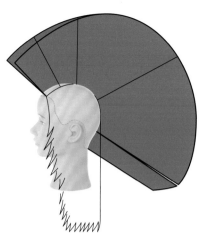

Lengths progress from the shortest at the forehead to the longest at the nape.

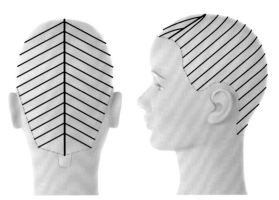

Diagonal-forward partings are used throughout, and all lengths are converged to a predetermined stationary design line to ensure perimeter length is not removed.

7 SCULPTING PROCEDURES

1. SECTION:
   (2) Side part to center nape

2. HEAD POSITION:
   Slightly forward

3. PART:
   Diagonal-forward

4. DISTRIBUTE: Perpendicular

5. PROJECT:
   Stationary design line 90°

6. FINGER/SHEAR POSITION: Parallel

7. DESIGN LINE:
   Diagonal-forward; stationary

DESIGN DECISIONS CHART

INCREASE-LAYERED FORM DIAGONAL-FORWARD LINE

Draw or fill in the boxes with the appropriate answers.

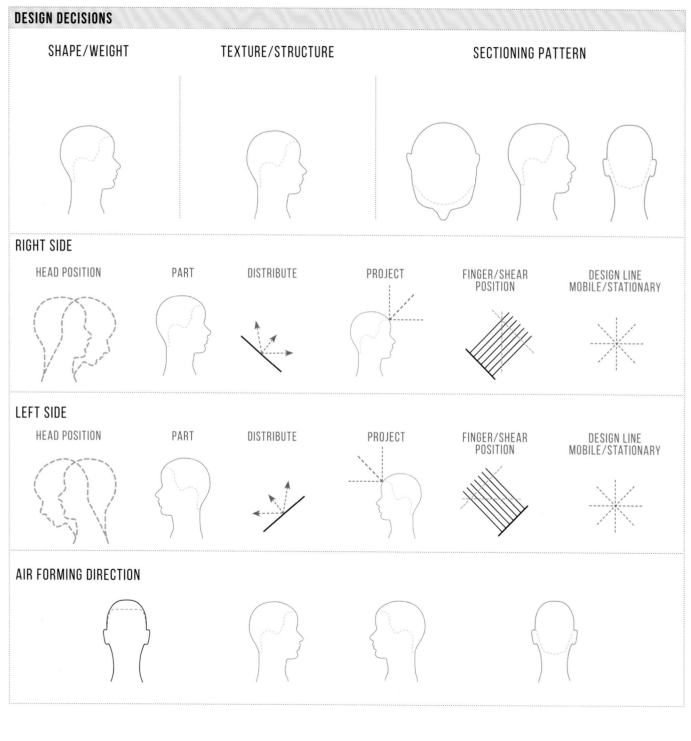

DESIGN DECISIONS

SHAPE/WEIGHT	TEXTURE/STRUCTURE	SECTIONING PATTERN

RIGHT SIDE

HEAD POSITION	PART	DISTRIBUTE	PROJECT	FINGER/SHEAR POSITION	DESIGN LINE MOBILE/STATIONARY

LEFT SIDE

HEAD POSITION	PART	DISTRIBUTE	PROJECT	FINGER/SHEAR POSITION	DESIGN LINE MOBILE/STATIONARY

AIR FORMING DIRECTION

Instructor Signature _____ Date _____

INCREASE-LAYERED FORM
DIAGONAL-FORWARD LINE

View the video, complete the Design Decisions chart, then perform this workshop. Complete the self-check as you progress through the workshop.

40 mins
Suggested
Salon Speed

PREPARATION		✔
	>> Assemble tools and products >> Set up workstation	☐

SECTIONING/HEAD POSITION/LENGTH GUIDE

	1. **Section hair into 2 areas:** >> Side part to center crown >> Center crown to center nape 2. **Position head upright.**	☐
	3. **Sculpt length guide using tip of nose as reference point.**	☐
	4. **Match sideburn, crown and nape lengths with length guide to ensure a pure increase-layered form.**	☐

RIGHT (HEAVIER) SIDE

	5. **Tilt head slightly forward.** 6. **Sculpt stationary design line on heavier side:** >> Diagonal-forward parting >> Perpendicular distribution >> Project 90° from curve of the head >> Parallel finger/shear position >> Sculpt parallel to parting	☐ ☐

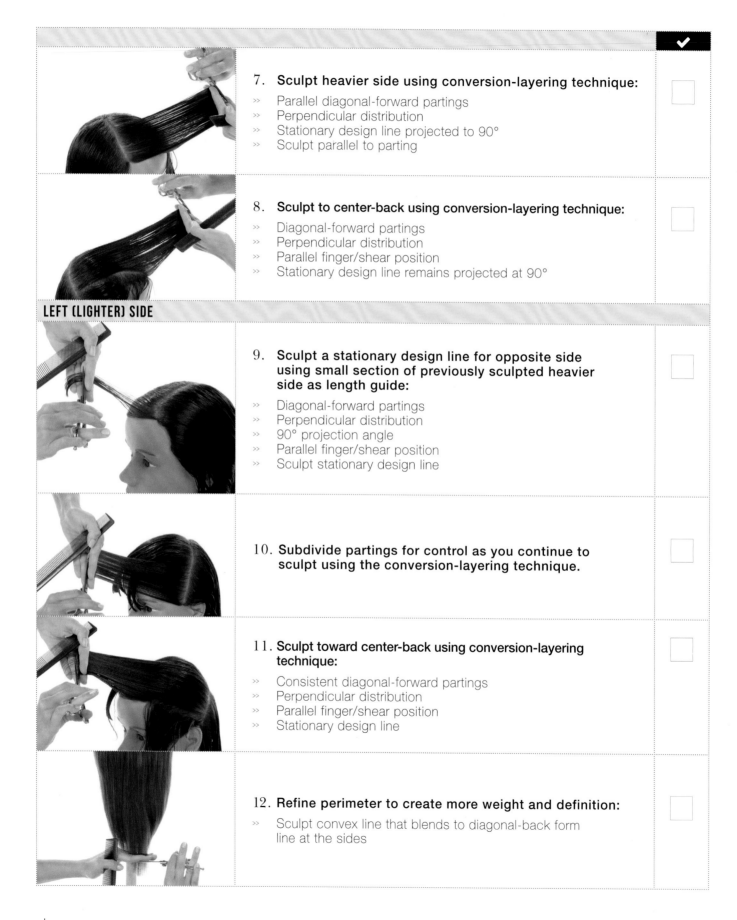

7. **Sculpt heavier side using conversion-layering technique:**
   >> Parallel diagonal-forward partings
   >> Perpendicular distribution
   >> Stationary design line projected to 90°
   >> Sculpt parallel to parting

8. **Sculpt to center-back using conversion-layering technique:**
   >> Diagonal-forward partings
   >> Perpendicular distribution
   >> Parallel finger/shear position
   >> Stationary design line remains projected at 90°

LEFT (LIGHTER) SIDE

9. **Sculpt a stationary design line for opposite side using small section of previously sculpted heavier side as length guide:**
   >> Diagonal-forward partings
   >> Perpendicular distribution
   >> 90° projection angle
   >> Parallel finger/shear position
   >> Sculpt stationary design line

10. **Subdivide partings for control as you continue to sculpt using the conversion-layering technique.**

11. **Sculpt toward center-back using conversion-layering technique:**
   >> Consistent diagonal-forward partings
   >> Perpendicular distribution
   >> Parallel finger/shear position
   >> Stationary design line

12. **Refine perimeter to create more weight and definition:**
   >> Sculpt convex line that blends to diagonal-back form line at the sides

AIR FORMING SCRUNCHING

13. Prepare hair for scrunching:

>> Dispense product into hand and gently rub palms together
>> Apply product through hair and distribute with a wide-tooth comb
>> Medium/high heat
>> Moderate airflow speed

Note: Increasing heat or airflow speed may result in a less-defined curl pattern and frizziness.

14. Tilt head back to allow hair to hang freely:

>> Position diffuser beneath exterior strands
>> Lift diffuser up into lengths

15. Dry ends, midstrand and then base:

>> Lift hair at scalp with your fingers
>> Excessively manipulating hair will result in less-defined curl pattern and frizziness
>> Proceed somewhat slowly from one area to next

16. Work toward the interior and complete back using same techniques.

17. Tilt head toward either side and use same techniques to dry hair:

>> Lift lengths gently
>> Work toward interior

18. Repeat on opposite side.

19. Finish style as desired.

COMPLETION ✔

>> Discard single-use supplies
>> Disinfect tools and multi-use supplies
>> Disinfect workstation and arrange in proper order

40 mins
Suggested Salon Speed

My Speed
——————
——————
——————

INSTRUCTIONS

Record your time in comparison with the suggested salon speed. Then, list here how you could improve your performance.

_____

_____

_____

_____

_____

VARIATION – INCREASE-LAYERED FORM, DIAGONAL-FORWARD LINE – CURLY HAIR

A variation on the increase-layered form, diagonal-forward line adapted to suit clients with curly hair is available online.

INCREASE-LAYERED FORM
HORIZONTAL LINE

EXPLORE

What do a staircase and a musical scale have in common?

INSPIRE

The conversion layering technique—easy as one, two, three—helps you create a pure increase-layered form.

ACHIEVE

Following this *Increase-Layered Form, Horizontal Line Workshop*, you'll be able to:

>> Identify the 7 Sculpting Procedures related to the increase-layered form along horizontal partings

>> Sculpt a balanced increase-layered form along horizontal partings using the conversion-layering technique

>> Air form increase-layered lengths along diagonal-back partings using a vent brush

Layered lengths disperse equally around the head.

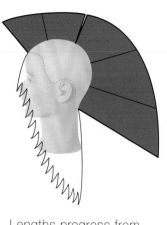

Lengths progress from shorter in the interior to longer in the exterior.

A center panel serves as a length guide. Horizontal partings are used throughout.

7 SCULPTING PROCEDURES

1. SECTION:
   (4) Center panel; ear to ear; crown to nape hairline

2. HEAD POSITION: Upright

3. PART: Horizontal

4. DISTRIBUTE: Perpendicular

5. PROJECT: Straight up

6. FINGER/SHEAR POSITION: Parallel

7. DESIGN LINE: Horizontal; stationary

INCREASE-LAYERED FORM HORIZONTAL LINE

Draw or fill in the boxes with the appropriate answers.

DESIGN DECISIONS

SHAPE / WEIGHT	TEXTURE / STRUCTURE	SECTIONING PATTERN

FRONT / SIDES

HEAD POSITION	PART	DISTRIBUTE	PROJECT	FINGER/SHEAR POSITION	DESIGN LINE MOBILE/STATIONARY

BACK

HEAD POSITION	PART	DISTRIBUTE	PROJECT	FINGER/SHEAR POSITION	DESIGN LINE MOBILE/STATIONARY

AIR FORMING DIRECTION

Instructor Signature _____   **Date** _____

PERFORMANCE GUIDE

INCREASE-LAYERED FORM HORIZONTAL LINE

View the video, complete the Design Decisions chart, then perform
this workshop. Complete the self-check as you progress through
the workshop.

40
mins
Suggested
Salon Speed

PREPARATION		✔
	» Assemble tools and products » Set up workstation	☐

SECTIONING – HEAD POSITION – LENGTH GUIDE

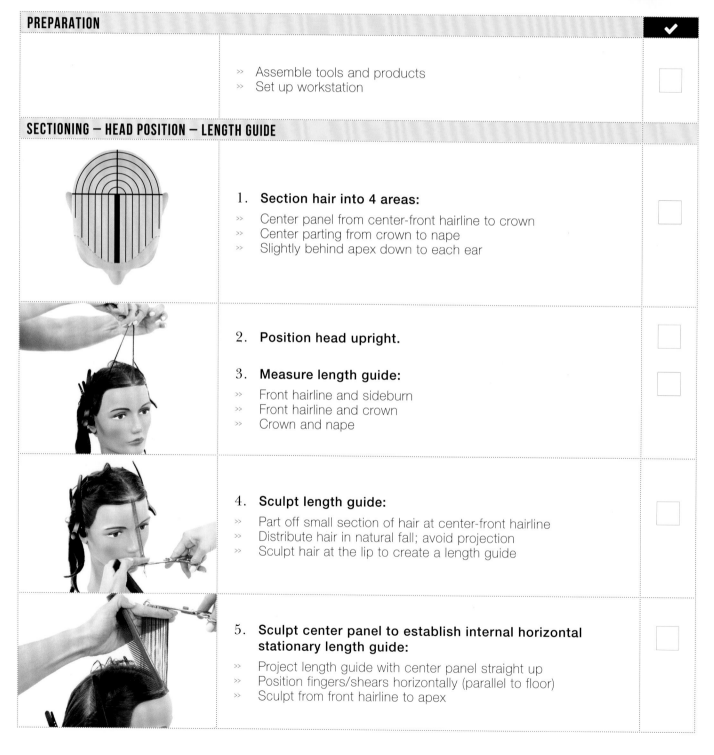	**1. Section hair into 4 areas:** » Center panel from center-front hairline to crown » Center parting from crown to nape » Slightly behind apex down to each ear	☐
	2. Position head upright.	☐
	3. Measure length guide: » Front hairline and sideburn » Front hairline and crown » Crown and nape	☐
	4. Sculpt length guide: » Part off small section of hair at center-front hairline » Distribute hair in natural fall; avoid projection » Sculpt hair at the lip to create a length guide	☐
	5. Sculpt center panel to establish internal horizontal stationary length guide: » Project length guide with center panel straight up » Position fingers/shears horizontally (parallel to floor) » Sculpt from front hairline to apex	☐

6. **Sculpt left side using conversion-layering technique:**
   » Stand opposite the side being sculpted
   » Horizontal parting
   » Distribute center panel straight up
   » Converge hair to horizontal stationary design line
   » Position fingers/shears horizontally (parallel to floor)
   » Sculpt on top of your fingers from front hairline toward back
   » Subdivide partings for control

7. **Continue to use conversion-layering technique:**
   » Horizontal partings
   » Subdivide partings for control

8. **Complete left side using same procedures:**
   » Work from top of section to bottom, subdividing partings for control

9. **Sculpt right side using conversion-layering technique:**
   » Stand opposite of side being sculpted
   » Horizontal partings
   » Distribute center panel straight up
   » Converge hair to stationary design line
   » Subdivide partings for control as you work from top of section to bottom

BACK – RIGHT SIDE

10. **Sculpt back-right side using conversion-layering technique:**
    » Use portion of previously sculpted top lengths as length guide
    » Horizontal partings
    » Position fingers/shears horizontally (parallel to floor)
    » Sculpt on top of your fingers

11. Subdivide partings for control and continue to use conversion-layering technique.

12. Work to hairline to complete back-right side.

BACK – LEFT SIDE

13. Sculpt back-left side using conversion-layering technique from horizontal partings:
   >> Stand opposite the length increase
   >> Use portion of previously sculpted top lengths as length guide
   >> Subdivide partings for control

14. Work toward the hairline to complete back-left side.

REFINE PERIMETER FORM LINE

15. Refine form line:
   >> Distribute hair in natural fall
   >> Notch entire form line to refine lengths as desired

AIR FORMING VENT BRUSH

16. **Apply mousse throughout hair.**

17. **Since form line of sculpture is diagonal-back, diagonal-back sections are used to air form lengths.**

18. **Air form hair beginning with shortest lengths at front hairline:**
    >> Use diagonal-back partings that extend slightly beyond center back
    >> Position vent brush parallel to partings
    >> Lift hair from base and use curved movement to create curved end texture
    >> Dry base, midstrand and ends

19. **Work toward back to complete this section using same air-forming procedures.**

20. **Continue to use same air-forming procedures:**
    >> Subdivide partings for control.

21. **In interior, use a higher projection angle to add volume.**

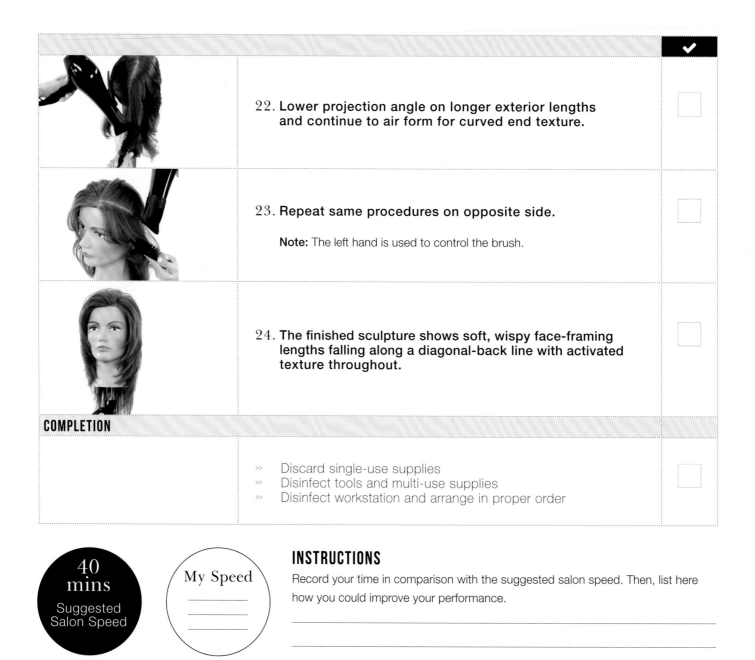

22. Lower projection angle on longer exterior lengths and continue to air form for curved end texture.

23. Repeat same procedures on opposite side.

    Note: The left hand is used to control the brush.

24. The finished sculpture shows soft, wispy face-framing lengths falling along a diagonal-back line with activated texture throughout.

COMPLETION

>> Discard single-use supplies
>> Disinfect tools and multi-use supplies
>> Disinfect workstation and arrange in proper order

40 mins
Suggested Salon Speed

My Speed
———
———
———

INSTRUCTIONS

Record your time in comparison with the suggested salon speed. Then, list here how you could improve your performance.

_____

_____

_____

_____

_____

VARIATION — INCREASE-LAYERED FORM — PLANAR SCULPTING

A variation on the increase-layered form, using the planar sculpting technique from horizontal partings, is available online.

105ᶜ.15
UNIFORMLY LAYERED FORM OVERVIEW

EXPLORE //

When you think of a round shape, what images come to mind?

INSPIRE //

Mastering the uniformly layered form will allow you to sculpt consistent lengths across the curves of the head.

ACHIEVE //

Following this *Uniformly Layered Form Overview*, you'll be able to:

>> Identify the characteristics of uniformly layered form

>> Explain the 7 Sculpting Procedures related to uniformly layered form

>> Give examples of sculpting guidelines for uniformly layered form

FOCUS //

UNIFORMLY LAYERED FORM OVERVIEW

Uniformly Layered Form Characteristics

Uniformly Layered Form Sculpting Procedures

Uniformly Layered Form Guidelines

The uniformly layered form is the true "one-length cut." In other words, all the lengths are uniform. Despite how simple this sculpture may appear, sculpting this form accurately takes skill and precision. The results are consistent layers and a rounded silhouette throughout. A uniformly layered form is sometimes referred to as a layered cut or 90° angle cut.

UNIFORMLY LAYERED FORM CHARACTERISTICS

SHAPE

» Uniformly layered forms are characterized by a rounded shape that parallels the curve of the head, resulting in a circular shape.

» There is no discernible weight within the form.

TEXTURE

» The sculpted texture of a uniformly layered form is totally activated.

» Curl patterns—whether natural or styled—will accentuate the surface texture, adding volume and dimension.

STRUCTURE

» All lengths are equal.

» Usually fall into the short- to mid-length category, but possible at longer lengths too.

» Color-coded green.

SALON**CONNECTION**

The True One-Length Cut

Some clients might request a one-length cut and really want a solid form or bob. They are picturing all of their hair falling to one place, perhaps their shoulders. You on the other hand may be envisioning a uniformly layered form. Be sure to ask specific questions during the consultation to ensure you achieve the look the client truly desires.

UNIFORMLY LAYERED FORM SCULPTING PROCEDURES

Understanding and mastering the 7 Sculpting Procedures needed to achieve uniformly layered lengths will allow you to create predictable results.

SECTION (1)

Section for control. Common sectioning lines are:

>> Center part; ear to ear across apex of the head

>> Subdividing interior between design line changes

HEAD POSITION (2)

The head is most often positioned upright. It can be positioned forward when layering in the nape.

PART (3)

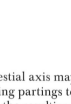

Any line from the celestial axis may be used. When choosing partings to sculpt uniform layers, the resulting texture will be influenced by the parting pattern chosen. Horizontal lines create weight, vertical lines create weightlessness and diagonal lines imply movement.

HORIZONTAL

In this example horizontal partings are used throughout the top of the head.

VERTICAL AND/OR PIVOTAL PARTINGS

>> In the first example, vertical partings in the front are combined with pivotal partings in the back.

>> In the second example, pivotal partings are used throughout the interior.

Partings should be controllable, and allow the design line to remain visible at all times. Partings that are too thick will make it difficult to see the design line, and it may be difficult to maintain a consistent projection angle.

DISTRIBUTE (4)

Perpendicular distribution is used to sculpt uniform lengths.

PROJECT (5)

>> A consistent 90° projection across the curve of the head.

>> Avoid inconsistent projection, which leads to uneven lengths.

>> Frequently check for accuracy while sculpting.

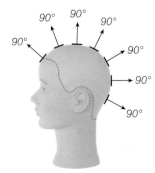

FINGER/SHEAR POSITION (6)

Position your fingers and shears parallel to the parting and to the curves of the head. Inconsistent finger positioning leads to uneven lengths.

PALM UP   PALM DOWN

The palm may face up or down, depending on the area of the head being sculpted.

On shorter lengths, you may choose to extend your little finger and rest it on the scalp to maintain equal distance from the head.

DESIGN LINE (7)

>> Any line from the celestial axis may be used to sculpt the design line.

>> A mobile design line is used to sculpt uniform lengths.

>> Each sculpted parting becomes the new design line for the next parting.

>> Keep the design line visible by using thin partings and following a consistent procedure.

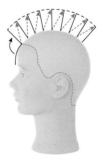

UNIFORMLY LAYERED FORM GUIDELINES

NONPARALLEL FINGER POSITION

>> Some head shapes may require adapting the technique to create the rounded silhouette.

>> In areas that are flatter, a nonparallel, more curved finger position may be used to compensate.

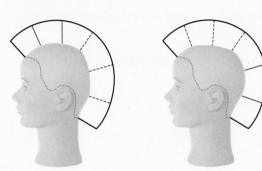

FORM VARIATIONS

Another option for creating uniform layers is to sculpt a design line in natural fall first, along the perimeter hairline. This design line can then be used as a guide to sculpt uniform lengths throughout. Sculpting in this manner creates a pure uniformly layered form with no weight at the perimeter.

  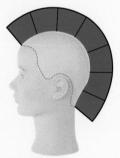

Sculpting a larger section along the perimeter hairline in natural fall establishes more weight. Then the uniformly layered lengths are sculpted using the weight corner as a guide.

 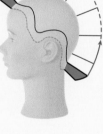 

Another way to sculpt a uniformly layered form is to begin sculpting the desired length in the interior and work toward the exterior. Then redefine the perimeter. This adds weight and customizes the form line.

TIGHTLY CURLED HAIR

An advanced technique, such as freeform sculpting, may be used when sculpting uniform layers on tightly curled hair. Although freeform sculpting does not include all 7 Sculpting Procedures, there are helpful guidelines that can lead to more predictable results.

» The tighter the curl pattern, the shorter the hair will appear after sculpting.

» In order to see the shape of the sculpture while creating it, position client in front of a light-colored background.

» Take a couple steps back frequently to judge the shape from a distance and at varying angles when sculpting.

DISCOVER**MORE**

A Roundabout Way
Did you know that a pure uniformly layered form is rare? Besides customizing the perimeter, uniform interiors are often combined with another basic form in the exterior. For instance, a combination form positioning increase layering in the exterior adds length and elongates the overall form. Positioning graduation in the exterior adds weight and expands the form where the two structures meet. Search the Internet to find both female and male images that include uniform lengths. Identify the other forms in the hair design and share your findings with your classmates.

The round shape of the uniformly layered form will be the perfect sculpture for some clients and is an important part of many combination forms.

LESSONS LEARNED

>> The characteristics of the uniformly layered form are:

- Shape – Rounded; echoes the shape of the head

- Texture – Activated; curl patterns increase expansion

- Structure – Equal lengths throughout

>> The 7 Sculpting Procedures related to uniformly layered form are:

1. Section with a center part and from ear to ear across the apex; or between design line changes.

2. Head position is generally upright.

3. Partings include horizontal, vertical and diagonal.

4. Distribution is perpendicular from the parting.

5. The projection angle is 90° from curves of head.

6. Finger/shear position is parallel to the parting and to the head.

7. A mobile design line is used throughout.

>> Additional guidelines for the uniformly layered form include:

- Sometimes it is necessary to use a nonparallel finger position in the flatter areas of the head to create the rounded silhouette.

- The perimeter form line can be sculpted first and used as a length guide for the remaining hair; or once the uniform layering has been sculpted, the form line then can be defined as desired.

- Freeform sculpting techniques can be used on tightly curled hair.

UNIFORMLY LAYERED FORM
HORIZONTAL/VERTICAL LINE

EXPLORE

The uniformly layered form is a highly requested sculpture in the salon. Why do you think it's so popular?

INSPIRE

The uniformly layered form is often requested because it's a versatile sculpture that can be finished in a variety of ways.

ACHIEVE

Following this *Uniformly Layered Form, Horizontal/Vertical Line Workshop*, you'll be able to:

>> Identify the 7 Sculpting Procedures related to the uniformly layered form, horizontal/vertical line

>> Sculpt a uniformly layered form with horizontal, vertical and pivotal partings, perpendicular distribution, and 90° projection

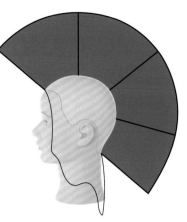

Uniform layers sculpted from horizontal, vertical and pivotal partings create a versatile sculpture that can be air formed for a variety of finishes.

Lengths are equal throughout the sculpture.

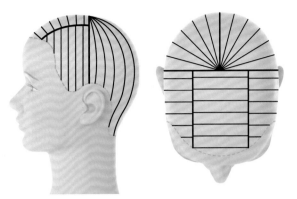

Horizontal partings are used in the top-center rectangle, which extends to the apex. The sides are sectioned from the corner of the rectangle to the top of the ear on each side, and the partings are vertical. Pivotal partings are taken in the remaining back section.

7 SCULPTING PROCEDURES

1. SECTION:
   (5) center-top rectangle; ear to ear; center parting from crown to nape hairline

2. HEAD POSITION: Upright

3. PART:
   Horizontal/Vertical/Pivotal

4. DISTRIBUTE: Perpendicular

5. PROJECT: 90°

6. FINGER/SHEAR POSITION: Parallel

7. DESIGN LINE:
   Horizontal/Vertical/Pivotal; mobile

DESIGN DECISIONS CHART

UNIFORMLY LAYERED FORM HORIZONTAL/VERTICAL LINE

Draw or fill in the boxes with the appropriate answers.

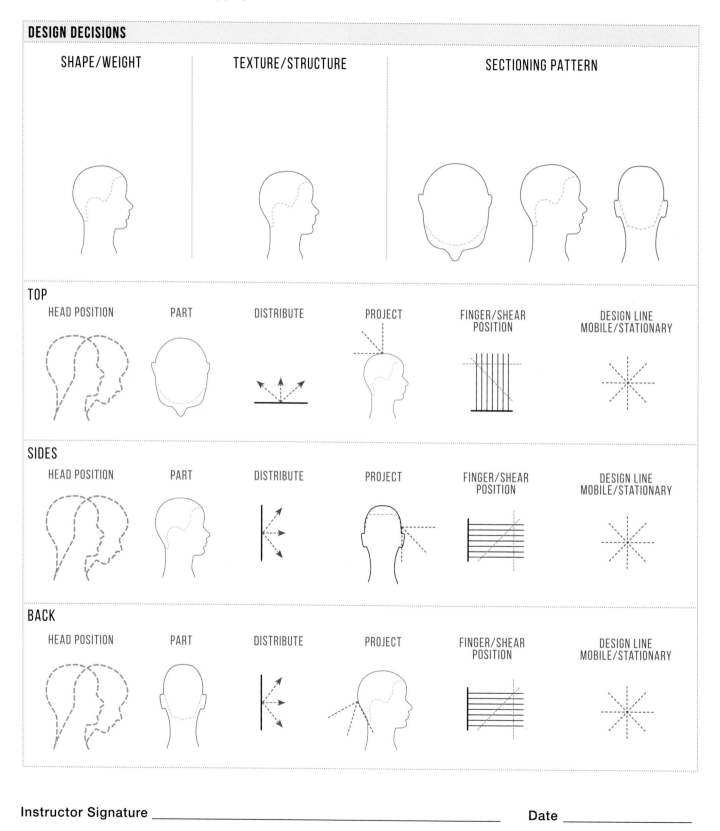

DESIGN DECISIONS

SHAPE/WEIGHT	TEXTURE/STRUCTURE	SECTIONING PATTERN

TOP

HEAD POSITION	PART	DISTRIBUTE	PROJECT	FINGER/SHEAR POSITION	DESIGN LINE MOBILE/STATIONARY

SIDES

HEAD POSITION	PART	DISTRIBUTE	PROJECT	FINGER/SHEAR POSITION	DESIGN LINE MOBILE/STATIONARY

BACK

HEAD POSITION	PART	DISTRIBUTE	PROJECT	FINGER/SHEAR POSITION	DESIGN LINE MOBILE/STATIONARY

Instructor Signature _____ **Date** _____

UNIFORMLY LAYERED FORM HORIZONTAL/VERTICAL LINE

View the video, complete the Design Decisions chart, then perform this workshop. Complete the self-check as you progress through the workshop.

20 mins
Suggested
Salon Speed

PREPARATION		✔
	» Assemble tools and products » Set up workstation	☐

SECTIONING – HEAD POSITION – LENGTH GUIDE

	1. **Section hair into 5 areas with a rectangle at top:** » Apex to each ear » Center of each eye at front hairline to apex » Apex to center nape	☐
	2. **Position head upright.**	☐
	3. **Sculpt length guide:** » Thin, horizontal parting at front hairline » Natural distribution » Parallel finger/shear position » Sculpt hair below lips	☐
	4. **Release and sculpt a horizontal parting at front hairline:** » Perpendicular distribution » 90° projection » Sculpt parallel to curve of head using length guide as mobile design line	☐
	5. **Sculpt remaining rectangle section from front hairline toward apex:** » Horizontal partings » Perpendicular distribution » 90° projection from curve of head » Parallel finger/shear position » Mobile design line	☐

SIDES

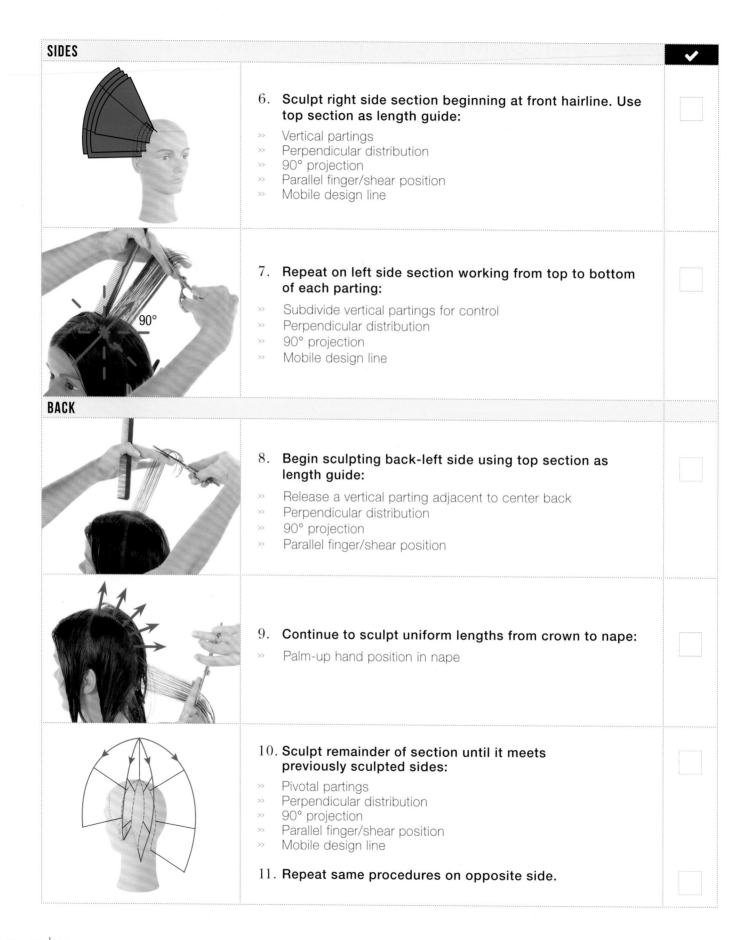

6. **Sculpt right side section beginning at front hairline. Use top section as length guide:**
   >> Vertical partings
   >> Perpendicular distribution
   >> 90° projection
   >> Parallel finger/shear position
   >> Mobile design line

7. **Repeat on left side section working from top to bottom of each parting:**
   >> Subdivide vertical partings for control
   >> Perpendicular distribution
   >> 90° projection
   >> Mobile design line

90°

BACK

8. **Begin sculpting back-left side using top section as length guide:**
   >> Release a vertical parting adjacent to center back
   >> Perpendicular distribution
   >> 90° projection
   >> Parallel finger/shear position

9. **Continue to sculpt uniform lengths from crown to nape:**
   >> Palm-up hand position in nape

10. **Sculpt remainder of section until it meets previously sculpted sides:**
    >> Pivotal partings
    >> Perpendicular distribution
    >> 90° projection
    >> Parallel finger/shear position
    >> Mobile design line

11. **Repeat same procedures on opposite side.**

		✔

12. Cross-check lengths in opposite direction of sculpted line:

» If lengths need to be refined, use original parting pattern

☐

REFINE PERIMETER FORM LINE

13. Refine perimeter form line using low projection.

☐

14. The finished sculpture shows an activated texture and a curvilinear shape.

☐

COMPLETION

» Discard single-use supplies
» Disinfect tools and multi-use supplies
» Disinfect workstation and arrange in proper order

☐

20 mins
Suggested Salon Speed

My Speed
_____
_____
_____

INSTRUCTIONS

Record your time in comparison with the suggested salon speed. Then, list here how you could improve your performance.

_____

_____

_____

_____

_____

UNIFORMLY LAYERED FORM
PIVOTAL LINE

EXPLORE

Do you think it will be easy to create a rounded form on shorter hair? Why?

INSPIRE

Using a pivotal parting pattern will help you follow the curves of the head when sculpting uniform layers.

ACHIEVE

Following this *Uniformly Layered Form, Pivotal Line Workshop*, you'll be able to:

» Identify the 7 Sculpting Procedures related to the uniformly layered form along pivotal partings

» Sculpt a balanced uniformly layered form using pivotal partings

» Air form shorter uniform lengths using the fingerstyling technique

» Air form shorter uniform lengths using a 9-row brush

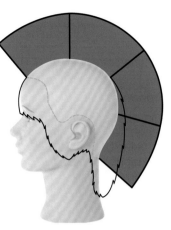

The rounded shape follows the curve of the head.

Lengths are uniform throughout the sculpture.

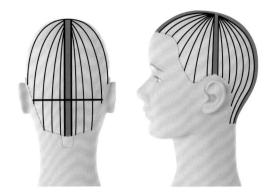

Center panels from the front hairline to the nape, and from the apex to each ear are sculpted first to serve as a length guide. Pivotal and vertical partings are used for the remainder of the sculpture.

7 SCULPTING PROCEDURES

1. SECTION:
   (4) Center front hairline to nape; apex to each ear

2. HEAD POSITION: Upright

3. PART: Pivotal; vertical

4. DISTRIBUTE: Perpendicular

5. PROJECT: 90°

6. FINGER/SHEAR POSITION: Parallel

7. DESIGN LINE:
   Pivotal/Vertical; mobile

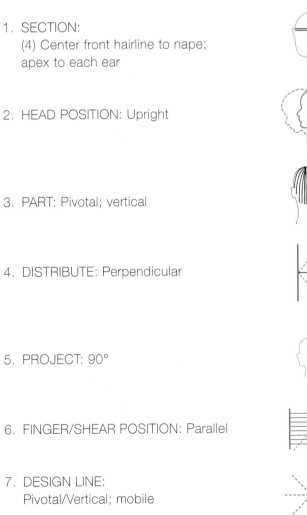

DESIGN DECISIONS CHART

UNIFORMLY LAYERED FORM PIVOTAL LINE

Draw or fill in the boxes with the appropriate answers.

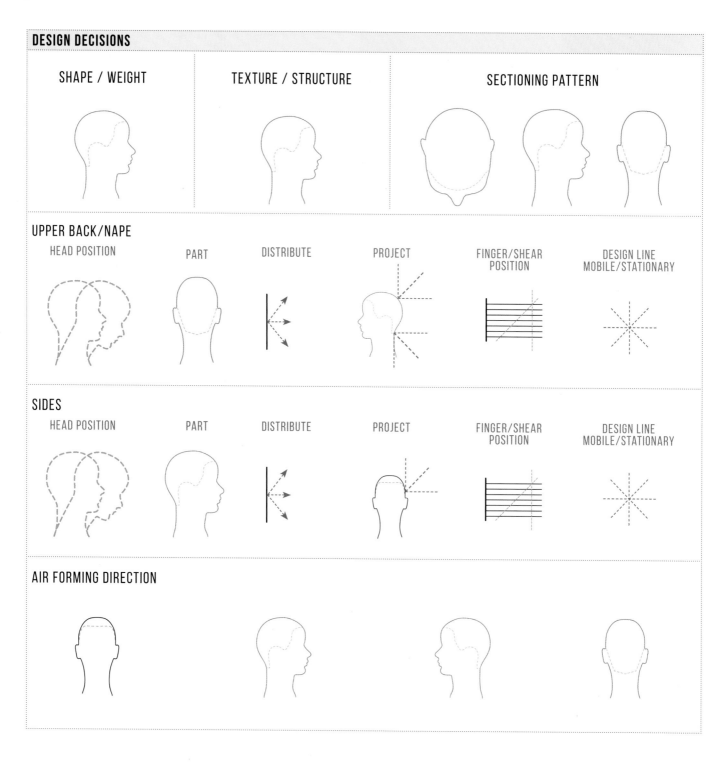

DESIGN DECISIONS

SHAPE / WEIGHT

TEXTURE / STRUCTURE

SECTIONING PATTERN

UPPER BACK/NAPE

HEAD POSITION | PART | DISTRIBUTE | PROJECT | FINGER/SHEAR POSITION | DESIGN LINE MOBILE/STATIONARY

SIDES

HEAD POSITION | PART | DISTRIBUTE | PROJECT | FINGER/SHEAR POSITION | DESIGN LINE MOBILE/STATIONARY

AIR FORMING DIRECTION

Instructor Signature _____ Date _____

UNIFORMLY LAYERED FORM PIVOTAL LINE

View the video, complete the Design Decisions chart, then perform
this workshop. Complete the self-check as you progress through
the workshop.

45 mins
Suggested
Salon Speed

PREPARATION ✔

>> Assemble tools and products
>> Set up workstation

☐

SECTIONING – HEAD POSITION – LENGTH GUIDE

1. **Section hair into 4 areas:**
   >> Part a panel from front hairline to nape
   >> Part a panel from apex to top of each ear

   ☐

2. **Position head upright.**

   ☐

3. **Sculpt length guide:**
   >> Part off small section of hair at center front hairline
   >> Distribute hair in natural fall; avoid projection
   >> Sculpt hair to the bridge of the nose to create a length guide

   ☐

4. **Sculpt center panel to establish internal length guide:**
   >> Project length guide with center panel to 90° from
      curve of head
   >> Position fingers/shears parallel to head
   >> Sculpt from front hairline to apex

   ☐

5. **Sculpt center panel from apex to nape:**
   >> 90° projection
   >> Parallel finger position

   ☐

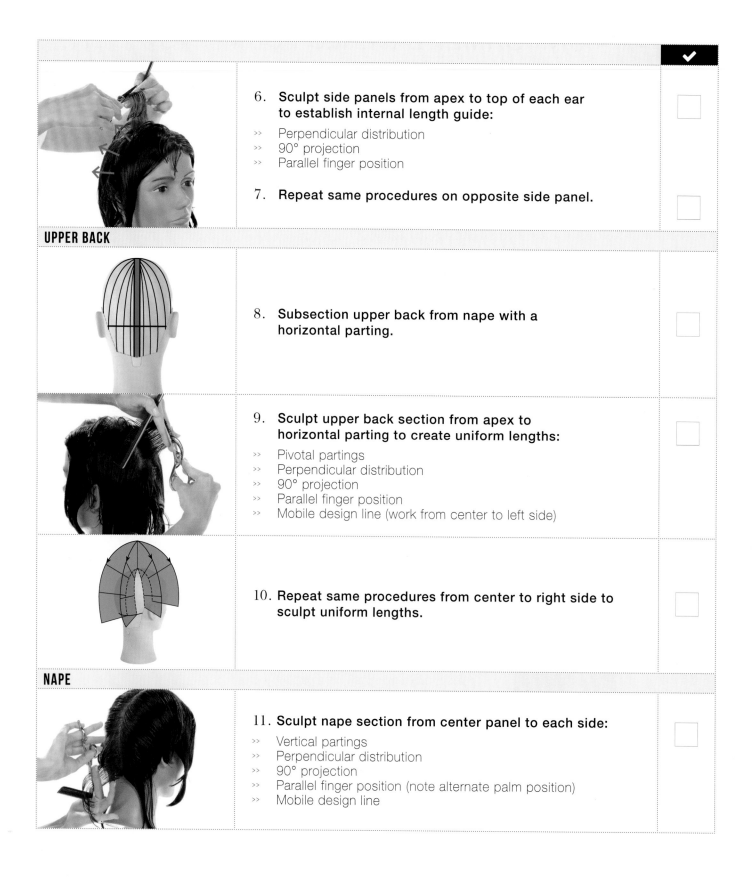

6. Sculpt side panels from apex to top of each ear to establish internal length guide:
   >> Perpendicular distribution
   >> 90° projection
   >> Parallel finger position

7. Repeat same procedures on opposite side panel.

UPPER BACK

8. Subsection upper back from nape with a horizontal parting.

9. Sculpt upper back section from apex to horizontal parting to create uniform lengths:
   >> Pivotal partings
   >> Perpendicular distribution
   >> 90° projection
   >> Parallel finger position
   >> Mobile design line (work from center to left side)

10. Repeat same procedures from center to right side to sculpt uniform lengths.

NAPE

11. Sculpt nape section from center panel to each side:
    >> Vertical partings
    >> Perpendicular distribution
    >> 90° projection
    >> Parallel finger position (note alternate palm position)
    >> Mobile design line

12. **Sculpt side section to create uniform lengths:**
    >> Pivotal partings
    >> Perpendicular distribution
    >> 90° projection
    >> Parallel finger position
    >> Mobile design line (work from top to side part)

13. **Repeat same procedures on opposite side to sculpt uniform lengths.**

14. **Check entire hair sculpture for symmetry and consistent uniform lengths.**

15. **Refine form line:**
    >> Air form hair
    >> Distribute hair in natural fall
    >> Personalize perimeter as desired

16. **The finished workshop shows a versatile rounded form, which can be finished in any direction allowing a wide range of styling options.**

AIR FORMING FINGERSTYLING

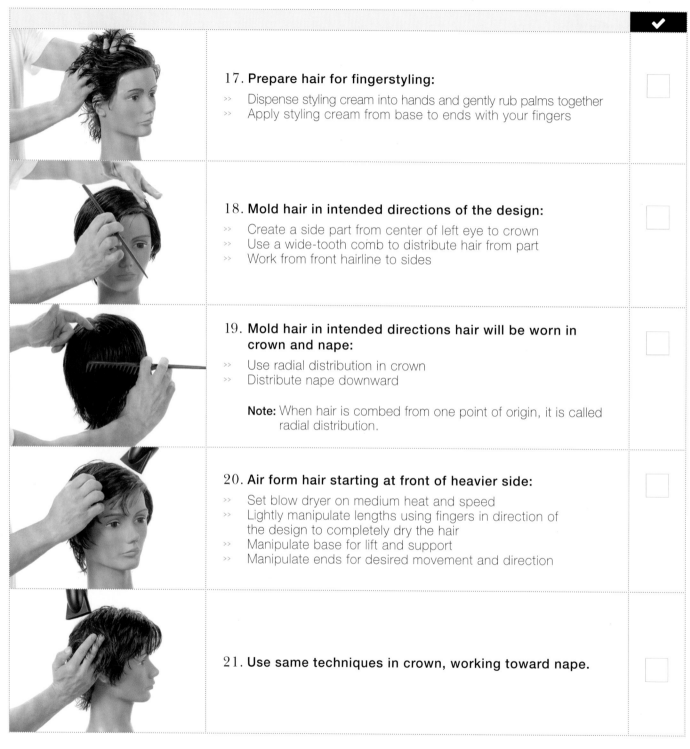

17. **Prepare hair for fingerstyling:**
    >> Dispense styling cream into hands and gently rub palms together
    >> Apply styling cream from base to ends with your fingers

18. **Mold hair in intended directions of the design:**
    >> Create a side part from center of left eye to crown
    >> Use a wide-tooth comb to distribute hair from part
    >> Work from front hairline to sides

19. **Mold hair in intended directions hair will be worn in crown and nape:**
    >> Use radial distribution in crown
    >> Distribute nape downward

    Note: When hair is combed from one point of origin, it is called radial distribution.

20. **Air form hair starting at front of heavier side:**
    >> Set blow dryer on medium heat and speed
    >> Lightly manipulate lengths using fingers in direction of the design to completely dry the hair
    >> Manipulate base for lift and support
    >> Manipulate ends for desired movement and direction

21. **Use same techniques in crown, working toward nape.**

22. Create a flipped-up effect (indentation) in nape and perimeter: » Direct airflow upward	☐
23. The finished air-formed lengths show a more casual, low-maintenance look.	☐

AIR FORMING 9-ROW BRUSH

24. As an option, a 9-row brush may be used to create additional volume and support after hair has been fingerstyled.	☐
25. Horizontal and diagonal-back brush positions are used in the back.	
26. Begin air forming just above center nape: » Position brush horizontally and air form from base to ends in curved movement	☐

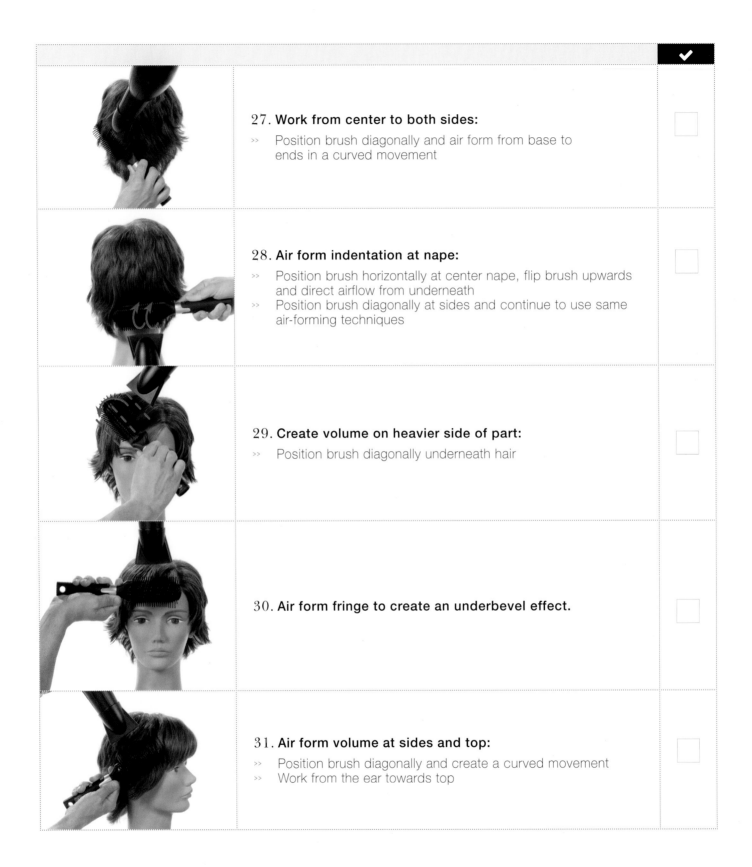

27. **Work from center to both sides:**
   >> Position brush diagonally and air form from base to ends in a curved movement

28. **Air form indentation at nape:**
   >> Position brush horizontally at center nape, flip brush upwards and direct airflow from underneath
   >> Position brush diagonally at sides and continue to use same air-forming techniques

29. **Create volume on heavier side of part:**
   >> Position brush diagonally underneath hair

30. **Air form fringe to create an underbevel effect.**

31. **Air form volume at sides and top:**
   >> Position brush diagonally and create a curved movement
   >> Work from the ear towards top

32. Air form indentation at side.

33. Repeat air-forming procedures on opposite side.

34. **Apply a silicone-based finishing product throughout the lengths to define and detail texture as desired.**

35. **The finished air-forming design shows a highly textured uniformly layered form that can be styled behind the ear.**

COMPLETION

>> Discard single-use supplies
>> Disinfect tools and multi-use supplies
>> Disinfect workstation and arrange in proper order

45 mins
Suggested Salon Speed

My Speed
_____
_____
_____

INSTRUCTIONS:

Record your time in comparison with the suggested salon speed. Then, list here how you could improve your performance.

_____
_____
_____
_____
_____

UNIFORMLY LAYERED FORM
VERTICAL/PIVOTAL LINE

EXPLORE

With curl patterns varying for every client, how could you make cutting textured hair easier and more accurate?

INSPIRE

Knowing how to adapt core sculpting techniques on various types of textures enhances your value as a hair designer.

ACHIEVE

Following this *Uniformly Layered Form, Vertical/Pivotal Line Workshop,* you'll be able to:

>> Identify the 7 Sculpting Procedures related to the uniformly layered form, vertical/pivotal line

>> Air form tightly curled hair straight using 9-row and round brushes

>> Dry sculpt a uniformly layered form using vertical and pivotal partings and the notching technique

The finish shows
uniform lengths,
which exhibit a
curvilinear shape.

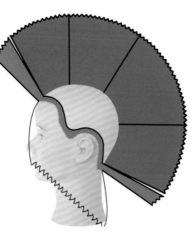

Uniform lengths blend
to a solid diagonal-back
perimeter.

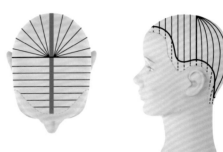

Vertical partings are used on the sides.
Pivotal partings are used in the back.
The perimeter is isolated and sculpted in
natural fall to establish a length guide. A
center vertical panel is used to establish an
additional length guide.

7 SCULPTING PROCEDURES

1. SECTION:
   4 sections; Center Panel,
   Perimeter Hairline

2. HEAD POSITION:
   Upright

3. PART:
   Vertical/Pivotal

4. DISTRIBUTE:
   Perpendicular

5. PROJECT:
   90°

6. FINGER/SHEAR POSITION:
   Parallel

7. DESIGN LINE:
   Vertical/Pivotal; mobile

DESIGN DECISIONS CHART

UNIFORMLY LAYERED FORM VERTICAL/PIVOTAL LINE

Draw or fill in the boxes with the appropriate answers.

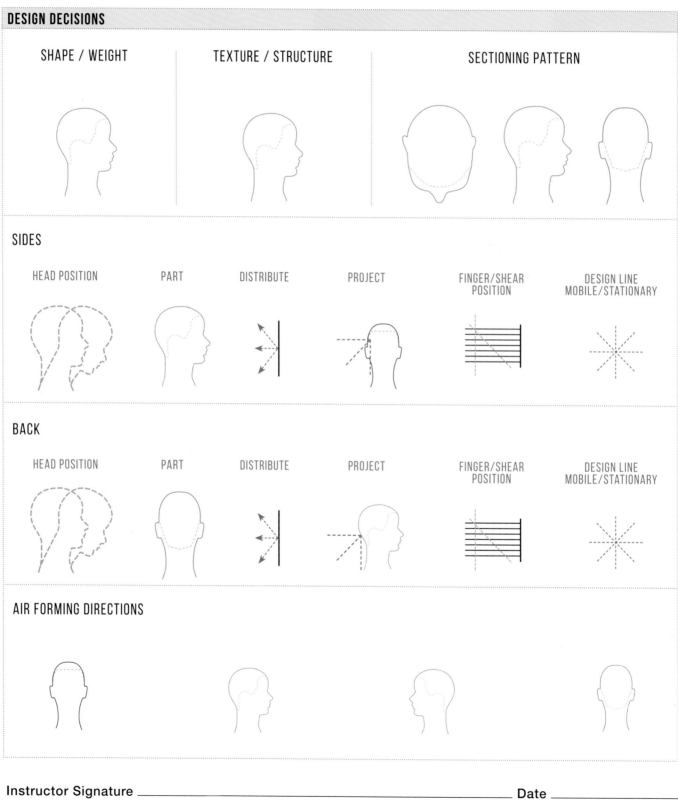

DESIGN DECISIONS

SHAPE / WEIGHT   TEXTURE / STRUCTURE   SECTIONING PATTERN

SIDES

HEAD POSITION   PART   DISTRIBUTE   PROJECT   FINGER/SHEAR POSITION   DESIGN LINE MOBILE/STATIONARY

BACK

HEAD POSITION   PART   DISTRIBUTE   PROJECT   FINGER/SHEAR POSITION   DESIGN LINE MOBILE/STATIONARY

AIR FORMING DIRECTIONS

Instructor Signature _____ **Date** _____

UNIFORMLY LAYERED FORM
VERTICAL/PIVOTAL LINE

View the video, complete the Design Decisions chart, then perform this workshop. Complete the self-check as you progress through the workshop.

1 hr 15 mins
Suggested
Salon Speed

PREPARATION	✔
» Assemble tools and products » Set up workstation	☐

SHAMPOO AND CONDITION, DETANGLE/SECTION

		✔
	1. **Shampoo and condition hair.**	☐
	2. **Detangle damp hair:** » Wide-tooth comb » Start at ends; work to base	☐
	3. **Section hair into 4 sections:** » Off-center parting to crown; crown to nape » Apex to back of each ear	☐
	4. **Apply thermal protectant product to each section:** » Subdivide with horizontal partings » Distribute through hair using wide-tooth comb	☐

AIR FORM – STRAIGHTEN CURL PATTERN

		✔
	5. **Horizontal partings are used in back and diagonal-back partings at sides to air form hair straight prior to cutting:** » Off-center parting	☐

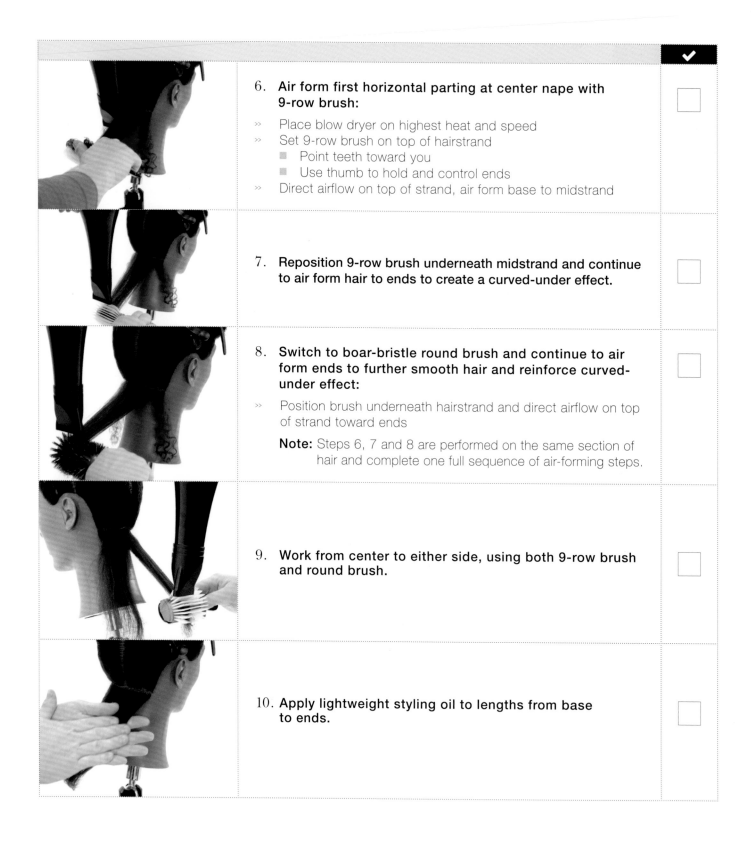

6. **Air form first horizontal parting at center nape with 9-row brush:**

   » Place blow dryer on highest heat and speed
   » Set 9-row brush on top of hairstrand
      ▪ Point teeth toward you
      ▪ Use thumb to hold and control ends
   » Direct airflow on top of strand, air form base to midstrand

7. **Reposition 9-row brush underneath midstrand and continue to air form hair to ends to create a curved-under effect.**

8. **Switch to boar-bristle round brush and continue to air form ends to further smooth hair and reinforce curved-under effect:**

   » Position brush underneath hairstrand and direct airflow on top of strand toward ends

   Note: Steps 6, 7 and 8 are performed on the same section of hair and complete one full sequence of air-forming steps.

9. **Work from center to either side, using both 9-row brush and round brush.**

10. **Apply lightweight styling oil to lengths from base to ends.**

11. Work up back using same air-forming procedures:

>> 9-row brush
>> Round brush
>> Subdivide partings for control
>> Apply lightweight styling oil to air-formed lengths from base to ends

12. Complete back section using same air-forming procedures.

13. Air form lighter side of part:

>> Diagonal-back partings
>> 9-row brush for smoothing surface
>> Round brush for curved-under effect
>> Apply lightweight styling oil to air-formed lengths from base to ends

14. Work up side section using same air-forming procedures.

15. Repeat on opposite side.

>> 9-row brush
>> Round brush

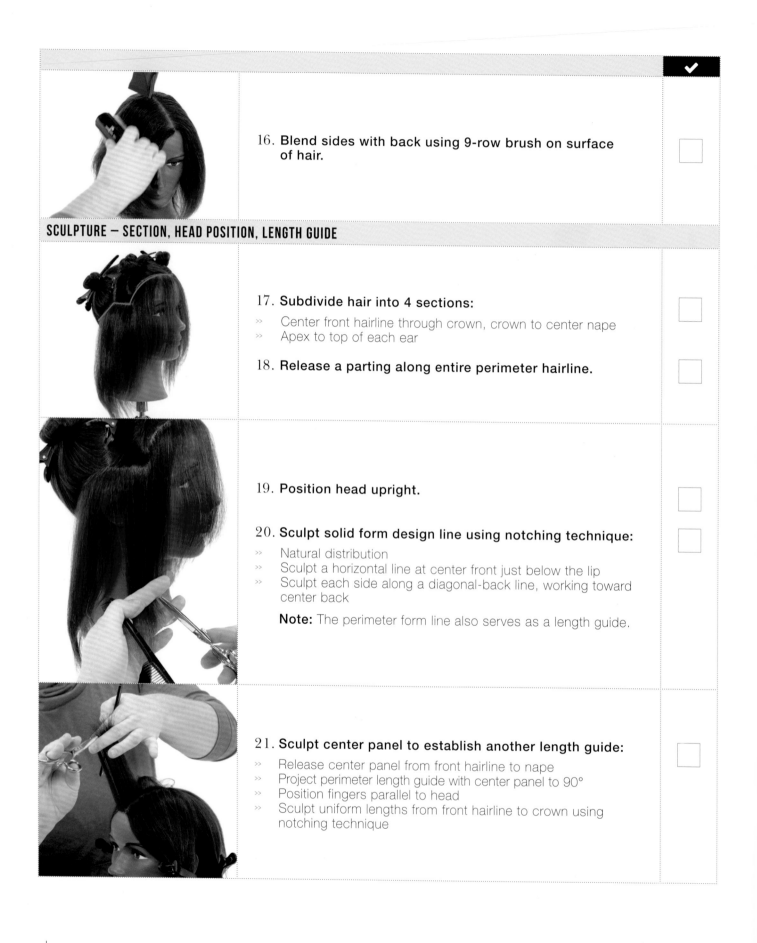

16. Blend sides with back using 9-row brush on surface of hair.

SCULPTURE — SECTION, HEAD POSITION, LENGTH GUIDE

17. Subdivide hair into 4 sections:
    >> Center front hairline through crown, crown to center nape
    >> Apex to top of each ear

18. Release a parting along entire perimeter hairline.

19. Position head upright.

20. Sculpt solid form design line using notching technique:
    >> Natural distribution
    >> Sculpt a horizontal line at center front just below the lip
    >> Sculpt each side along a diagonal-back line, working toward center back

    Note: The perimeter form line also serves as a length guide.

21. Sculpt center panel to establish another length guide:
    >> Release center panel from front hairline to nape
    >> Project perimeter length guide with center panel to 90°
    >> Position fingers parallel to head
    >> Sculpt uniform lengths from front hairline to crown using notching technique

22. **Continue to sculpt center panel from crown to nape using notching technique:**

>> Perpendicular distribution
>> 90° projection
>> Parallel finger position
>> Palm-up hand position in nape

SIDES

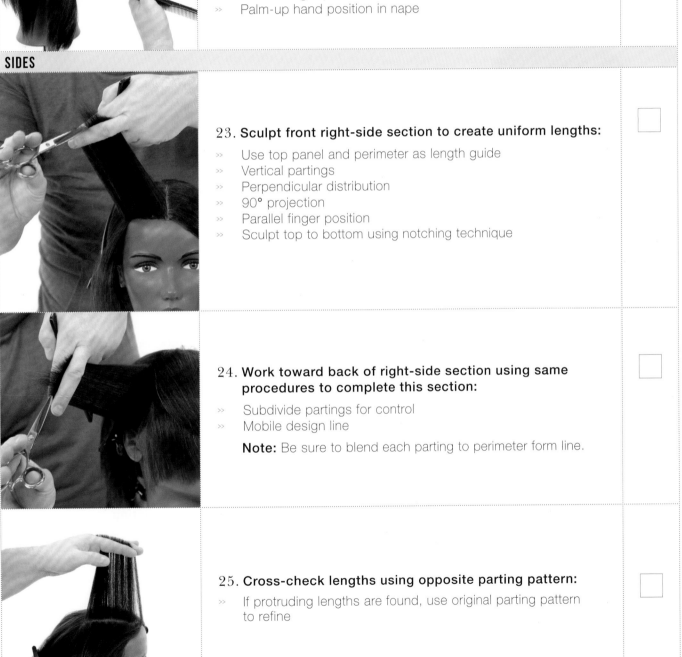

23. **Sculpt front right-side section to create uniform lengths:**

>> Use top panel and perimeter as length guide
>> Vertical partings
>> Perpendicular distribution
>> 90° projection
>> Parallel finger position
>> Sculpt top to bottom using notching technique

24. **Work toward back of right-side section using same procedures to complete this section:**

>> Subdivide partings for control
>> Mobile design line

Note: Be sure to blend each parting to perimeter form line.

25. **Cross-check lengths using opposite parting pattern:**

>> If protruding lengths are found, use original parting pattern to refine

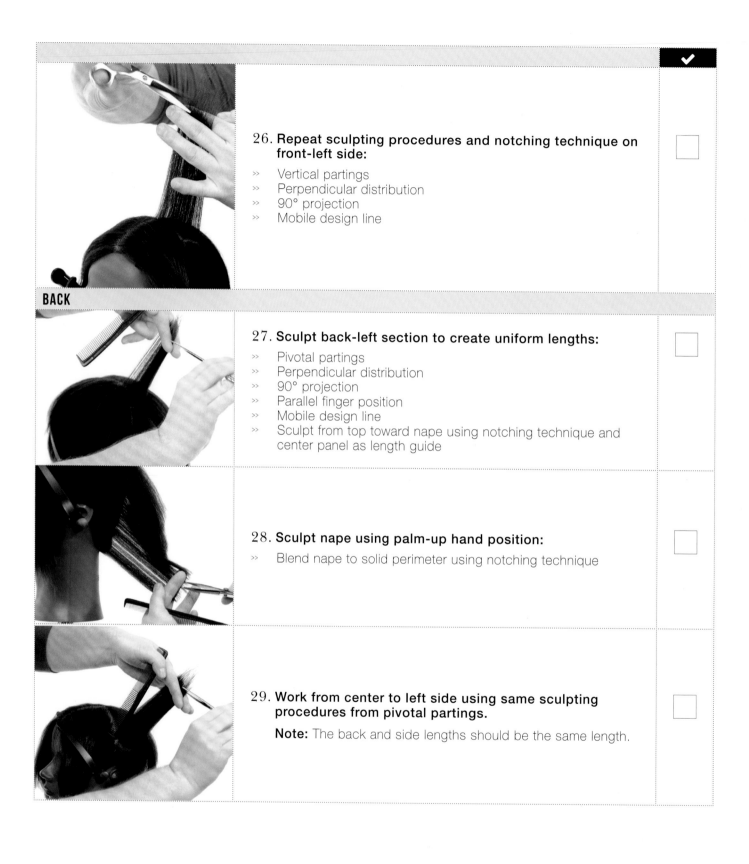

26. **Repeat sculpting procedures and notching technique on front-left side:**
    - » Vertical partings
    - » Perpendicular distribution
    - » 90° projection
    - » Mobile design line

BACK

27. **Sculpt back-left section to create uniform lengths:**
    - » Pivotal partings
    - » Perpendicular distribution
    - » 90° projection
    - » Parallel finger position
    - » Mobile design line
    - » Sculpt from top toward nape using notching technique and center panel as length guide

28. **Sculpt nape using palm-up hand position:**
    - » Blend nape to solid perimeter using notching technique

29. **Work from center to left side using same sculpting procedures from pivotal partings.**

    Note: The back and side lengths should be the same length.

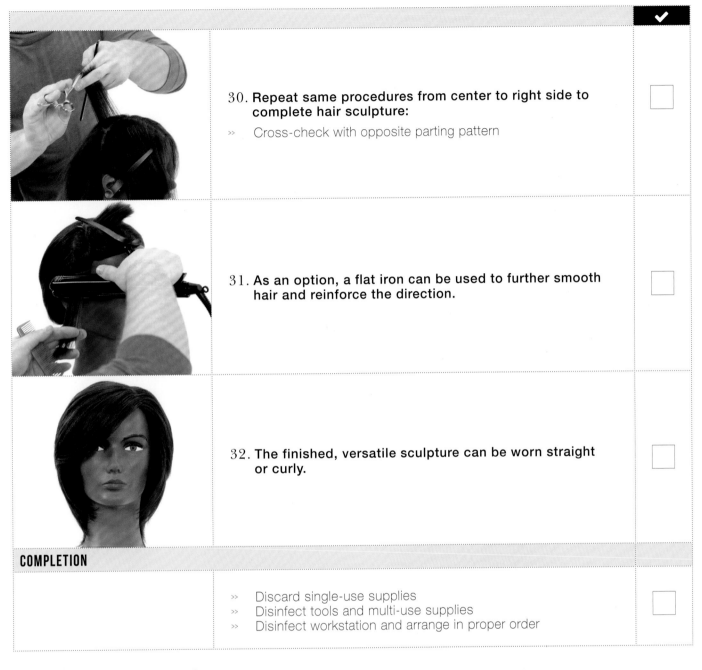

30. Repeat same procedures from center to right side to complete hair sculpture: » Cross-check with opposite parting pattern	☐
31. As an option, a flat iron can be used to further smooth hair and reinforce the direction.	☐
32. The finished, versatile sculpture can be worn straight or curly.	☐

COMPLETION

» Discard single-use supplies » Disinfect tools and multi-use supplies » Disinfect workstation and arrange in proper order	☐

1 hr 15 mins
Suggested
Salon Speed

My Speed
_____
_____
_____

INSTRUCTIONS:
Record your time in comparison with the suggested salon speed. Then, list here how you could improve your performance.

_____
_____
_____
_____
_____

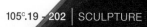

105ᶜ.19
TEXTURIZING TECHNIQUES

EXPLORE //

What are some different ways you can alter the edge of a piece of fabric? What effects do they create?

INSPIRE //

Personalized haircuts from sharp and jagged to soft and wispy are all possible with texturizing techniques.

ACHIEVE //

Following this lesson on *Texturizing Techniques*, you'll be able to:

>> Identify where texturizing can occur along the strand

>> List three categories of texturizing techniques

>> Provide examples of client-centered guidelines for texturizing

FOCUS //

TEXTURIZING TECHNIQUES

Texturizing Areas of the Strand

Texturizing Categories

Client-Centered Guidelines for Texturizing

105°.19 | TEXTURIZING TECHNIQUES

Texturizing techniques allow you to personalize hair sculptures for each unique client.

Texturizing involves sculpting shorter lengths within the form or along the perimeter without shortening the overall appearance of length. Texturizing is sometimes referred to as tapering or thinning since it is often used to reduce bulk and create closeness. Texturizing techniques can soften the ends of the hair and add mobility, texture, fullness and expansion.

Texturizing techniques can be performed:

>> During the hair sculpture on damp or dry hair

>> On dry curly hair for control and to observe the shrinkage factor

>> After the sculpture when you observe how the hair falls and responds

>> Throughout the entire sculpture to texturize the ends simultaneously as you create the overall form

Depending on the desired effect, texturizing techniques can be performed with a variety of tools, such as:

>> Shears

>> Taper shears (thinning shears)

>> Razor

>> Clippers

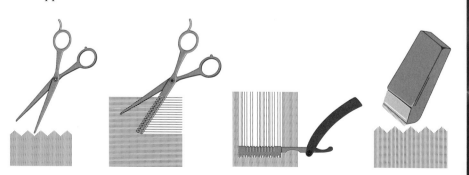

TEXTURIZING AREAS OF THE STRAND

Texturizing techniques can be performed at any of the three areas of the hairstrand:
>> Base
>> Midstrand
>> Ends

BASE

Up to 1" (2.5 cm) away from the scalp:

>> Creates expansion and fullness

>> Removes weight at the base area, allowing the hair to lift away from the head, creating volume

>> Shorter lengths support the longer lengths to encourage natural texture and movement

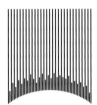

MIDSTRAND

Between the base area up to 1" (2.5 cm) before the ends:

>> Creates strand mobility

>> Reduces bulk and weight for a more contoured effect

>> Shorter lengths support the longer lengths to create fullness

END

Ends of the hair:

>> Creates end mobility

>> Softens the ends and helps to blend weight lines

>> Creates a specific end texture, such as chunky or soft depending on the tool used

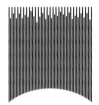

Natural Texture

Consider the hair's natural texture in order to determine where on the hairstrand to perform the technique.

FINE HAIR	MEDIUM HAIR	COARSE HAIR
Fine hair can be texturized as close as ½" (1.25 cm) from the scalp. >> Can be texturized closer to the scalp than coarse hair >> Needs the extra support of the shorter lengths underneath in order to achieve a fuller-looking effect	Medium hair should be texturized 1" (2.5 cm) away from the scalp.	Coarse hair should be texturized at least 1½" (3.75 cm) away from the scalp. >> If coarse hair is texturized too close to the scalp, the shorter lengths will not blend with the surface hair, creating an uneven, spiked effect

Avoid thinning around the hairline. Such thinning creates short, uneven hairs that are difficult to control.

TEXTURIZING CATEGORIES

Following are three main categories of texturizing and how they can be performed:

>> Form Line Tapering

>> Contour Tapering

>> Expansion Tapering

FORM LINE TAPERING

Form line tapering refers to texturizing the ends of the hair along the form line. It is also called end tapering and is used to:

>> Soften and blend weight lines

>> Reduce bulk and increase mobility of the hair

>> Add surface texture within the form and to the ends of the hair

Nine types of form line tapering are covered in this lesson:

1. Notching

2. Point Cutting

3. Slide Cutting

4. Slithering

5. End Tapering With Taper Shears

6. Razor Etching

7. Razor Peeling

8. Bevel-Up

9. Bevel-Under

Notching		
	>> Tips of shears are pointed into the ends creating a zigzag pattern	
	>> Creates irregular lengths, usually for a chunkier texture along the hair ends	
	>> Removes weight to encourage mobility	
	>> Can be used to sculpt the entire form or specific areas	
	>> Can be performed with shears or clippers	

Point Cutting (Pointing)		
	>> Tips of straight shears are inserted into the strands; movement is from finger position toward ends	
	>> Used to create irregular progression of lengths	
	>> Amount of end tapering depends on finger position and number of strokes	
	>> Releases weight and creates textural interest	

Slide Cutting		
	>> Slightly closed shears slide down the strand to produce a rapid length increase	
	>> Used for blending and framing areas around the hairline	
	>> Maintains maximum length and weight in forms	

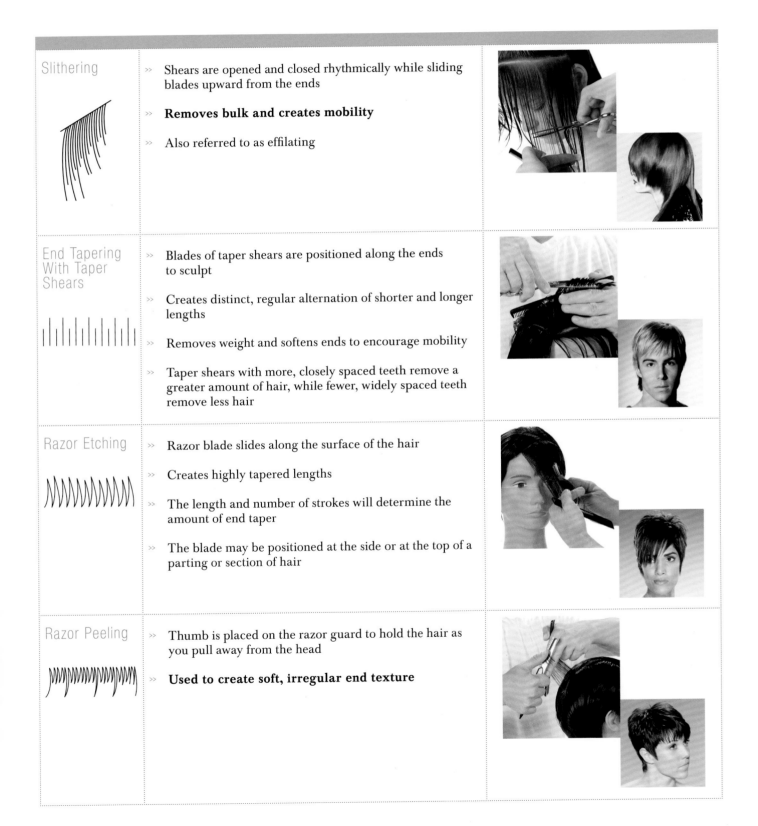

Slithering

>> Shears are opened and closed rhythmically while sliding blades upward from the ends

>> **Removes bulk and creates mobility**

>> Also referred to as effilating

End Tapering With Taper Shears

>> Blades of taper shears are positioned along the ends to sculpt

>> Creates distinct, regular alternation of shorter and longer lengths

>> Removes weight and softens ends to encourage mobility

>> Taper shears with more, closely spaced teeth remove a greater amount of hair, while fewer, widely spaced teeth remove less hair

Razor Etching

>> Razor blade slides along the surface of the hair

>> Creates highly tapered lengths

>> The length and number of strokes will determine the amount of end taper

>> The blade may be positioned at the side or at the top of a parting or section of hair

Razor Peeling

>> Thumb is placed on the razor guard to hold the hair as you pull away from the head

>> **Used to create soft, irregular end texture**

Bevel-Up	>> Razor blade is positioned on top of the section of hair and is moved in curved strokes with light pressure >> Produces a slight upward turn of the ends or "flip" >> The amount of flip you achieve is determined by the length of stroke and pressure applied	
Bevel-Under	>> Razor blade is positioned under the section of hair and the razor is moved in curved strokes >> Produces a slight turned-under effect at the ends >> The amount of pressure you use and the length of your strokes will influence the amount of end taper achieved	

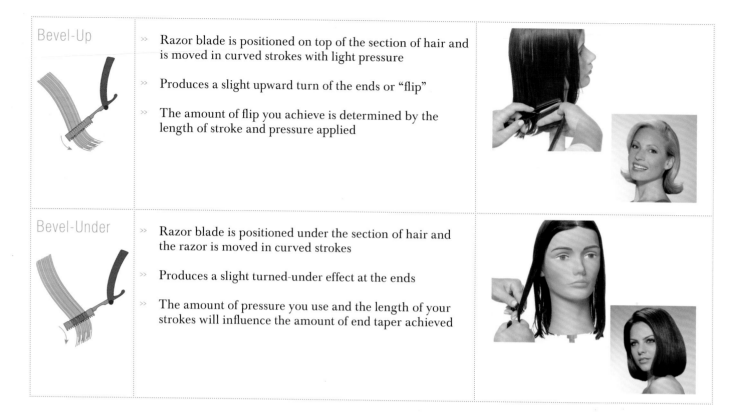

When texturizing with a razor, a very light stroke must be used to avoid a chunky effect.

DISCOVER**MORE**

Practice! Practice! Practice!

Texturizing techniques require much practice! There is only so much you can learn from books. Practicing with various texturizing tools on different hair textures will increase your skills to predict results. The confidence you will gain will fuel your creativity, allowing you to create limitless personalized designs for your clients. Search the Internet for various texturizing tools. Share your favorites with your classmates.

CONTOUR TAPERING

This texturizing technique is performed at the midstrand and ends to reduce bulk and allow the hair to lie closer to the head.

Taper-Shear-Over-Comb	» **Hair is controlled with a comb and sculpted with the taper shears** » **Lengths are softened and blended**	
Razor Rotation	» Performed by rotating the razor and the comb in a light, circular motion to reduce bulk and blend the form » **Used to create soft end texture and mobility** » **Hair should be damp when performing razor rotation in order to avoid client discomfort**	

EXPANSION TAPERING

The expansion tapering technique is usually performed near the base or midstrand to create expansion and volume. It removes weight throughout the strand, allowing the hair to lift away from the head. The shorter lengths support the longer lengths.

Strand Tapering With Taper Shears	» Taper shears are positioned diagonally » Creates expansion and volume within the form » Reduces bulk along the strand » The more times you close the shears the greater the amount of hair removed	
Slicing	» Performed by gliding the open shears along the surface of the hair » Used to create mobility and expansion » The amount of texture activation is controlled by how wide the shears are opened and the length of the stroke	

CLIENT-CENTERED GUIDELINES FOR TEXTURIZING

Client-centered guidelines are designed to help you do everything possible to enhance your client's comfort during the service and satisfaction after the service. Combining your knowledge plus practical experience will help you grow and maintain a loyal clientele.

TEXTURIZING TECHNIQUE TIPS

Notching	
	» The depth of the notch can range from shallow—for a soft, diffused line—to deep for a chunkier end texture.
	» With each parting, be sure to position your fingers at a constant distance from the ends. This will ensure consistent end texture.

Point Cutting (Pointing)	
	» Keep hair evenly damp.
	» Do not open shears all the way while point cutting.
	» Avoid using dull shears, which could cause pulling and client discomfort when point cutting.

Razor Etching	
	» Ensure hair is evenly damp.
	» Use a sharp razor and change the blade frequently.
	» Ensure that the blade of the razor touches the hair at a slight angle; use even, fluid strokes to remove the hair.
	» Choose longer strokes for more end texture.
	» Choose shorter strokes for less end texture.

Razor Peeling	
	» Ensure hair is evenly damp.
	» Use a razor with a guard; position thumb on top of guard and pull razor away from strand.
	» If less end texture is desired, position blade closer to the ends before peeling.
	» For more end texture, position the blade farther away from the ends before peeling.

Texturizing techniques involve sculpting shorter lengths within the form. Texturizing techniques can be performed during the sculpture, as a final phase of the sculpture, or even after you have dried the hair to personalize the form.

LESSONS LEARNED

» Texturizing is positioned along three areas of the hairstrand:

- Base

- Midstrand

- Ends

» Three categories of texturizing techniques include:

- Form Line Tapering

- Contour Tapering

- Expansion Tapering

» Client-centered guidelines for texturizing include:

- Keeping the hair evenly damp when using the razor

- Using a sharp razor and changing the blade frequently

- Using fluid, even strokes when razor etching

- When notching, let the design line extend through your fingers—at least equal to the depth of your notching stroke—to ensure that lengths don't gradually increase

105ᶜ.20 //
COMBINATION FORM
OVERVIEW

EXPLORE //

What are some objects created by the combination of two or more of the three basic shapes—the circle, triangle and square?

FOCUS //

COMBINATION FORM OVERVIEW

Combination Form Characteristics

Proportional Relationships

INSPIRE //

Create any hair shape you can imagine by combining two or more of the four basic forms.

ACHIEVE //

Following this *Combination Form Overview*, you'll be able to:

>> Describe the characteristics that each basic form adds to a combination form

>> List factors to consider when determining the proportional relationship within a combination form

105ᶜ.20 |
COMBINATION FORM OVERVIEW

combination form displays the characteristics of each form. When combining forms, careful consideration is given to the proportional relationship, or amount of one form in relation to the other form.

COMBINATION FORM CHARACTERISTICS

Most often, you will combine forms to position a specific shape, add weight or elongate the form. This means that you may sculpt one form in one area and another form in another area of the design. When combining forms, be aware of the qualities of each form and what each one adds to the overall design.

SHAPE/TEXTURE/STRUCTURE

The shape, texture and structure of a combination form depends on the proportions used and the length each form is sculpted.

>> Shape – The silhouette of a combination form will reveal the overall shape or shapes within a sculpture. Think of combination forms as shape on shape:

- Solid – Square/rectangular
- Graduated – Triangle/angular
- Increase – Oval/elongated
- Uniform – Circle/rounded

>> Texture – The surface texture reflects the combination of forms, and the length at which they are sculpted. Depending on the length of the interior layers, the surface textures can appear to be totally or partially activated. The shorter the layering, the more activated the texture.

>> Structure – The length arrangement of a combination form is the result of the position—interior versus exterior—of the forms combined.

Keep the following in mind when sculpting combination forms:

>> The hair is sectioned according to changes in desired line, shape and structure.

>> Position solid form in the exterior to add weight along the perimeter form line and to create a rectangular shape.

>> Position graduated forms in the exterior to create expansion and an angular shape.

>> Position increase layering in the exterior to elongate the overall form and to create an oval shape.

>> Position uniform layers in the interior to add volume and to create a rounded shape.

SALON**CONNECTION**

Compose and Personalize

In the salon, most hair sculptures are combination forms. What will set you apart from many stylists will be your ability to compose and personalize designs. Once you learn the characteristics of each form and what to expect with different combinations, you will be able to compose endless possibilities. Use texturizing techniques to personalize and add your signature touch for each client.

Increase/Solid

>> Increase layering in the interior adds volume and softens the rectangular shape of a solid form.

>> A solid exterior adds weight to the perimeter form line.

>> Shorter increase layers sculpted over solid form create an overall activated texture.

Increase/Solid

>> A longer increase in the front creates face-framing softness, and the solid form in the back creates unactivated surface texture with perimeter weight.

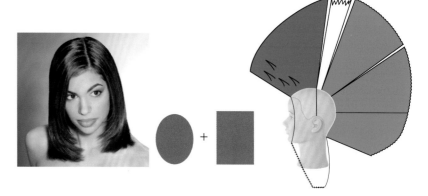

Increase/Graduated

>> Increase layering adds texture and elongates the form from the top of the head toward the crown and from the top of the head toward the fringe.

>> High graduation sculpted in the exterior shifts the weight toward the crown.

>> Consider the position of weight, which will create expansion when designing this combination form.

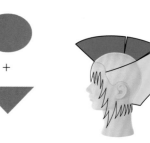

Graduated/Increase

The reverse combination of graduation over increase-layered texture can also be sculpted.

>> Longer graduated lengths create an unactivated surface texture in the interior.

>> Interior weight contrasts with increase-layered lengths that elongate the form and create a close-fitting contour.

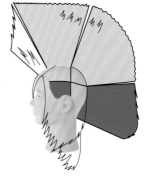

Uniform/Graduated

>> Uniform interior lengths create a totally activated, rounded silhouette.

>> A graduated exterior creates an angular silhouette and expansion at the occipital area.

Uniform/Graduated

>> Be aware of the weight area that occurs and where it falls relative to the client's features.

>> Consider the line of inclination– low, medium or high–when designing this combination form.

 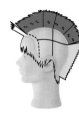

Uniform/Increase

>> Uniform lengths in the interior create a rounded shape that conforms to the curve of the head.

>> The increase-layered exterior elongates the form.

>> The surface texture of the uniformly layered portion is totally activated, while the increase-layered portion has a more spread-out activated appearance.

Square (Rectilinear) Form

>> A square form is created using the planar sculpting technique.

>> A weight area is created where the increase-layered form meets the graduated form in the crown.

DISCOVER**MORE**

Shaping Up Design

Did you know that nature automatically creates "shape-on-shape" designs? Artists gain inspiration from nature when composing their works of art. You can also borrow inspiration from nature and the arts to compose your unique designs. Search the Internet for images from nature and the arts to gain inspiration for shape-on-shape compositions.

PROPORTIONAL RELATIONSHIPS

Proportional relationships determine the sectioning and sculpting techniques to be used. Consider the following when deciding on the proportional relationship of one form to another, which will affect the overall resulting shape and position of expansion within the form:

›› Placement of desired weight relative to head shape

›› Placement of desired weight relative to facial features

›› Proportion of desired weight to surface texture

Increase/Solid

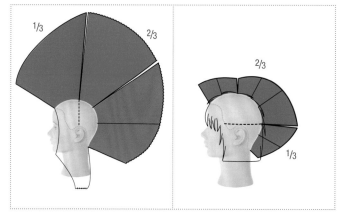

Uniform/Graduated

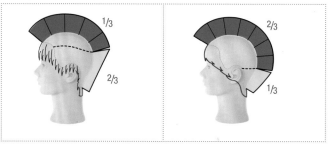

Uniform/Increase

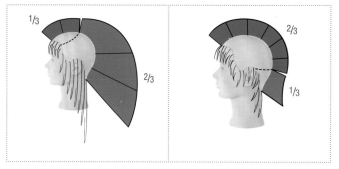

Combination form possibilities are endless, and it is not uncommon to sculpt three or four forms within one sculpture. Let your imagination be your guide when composing combination forms.

Once you understand how to combine forms, you will have the option of blending one form to another, or disconnecting the shapes, depending on the desired results.

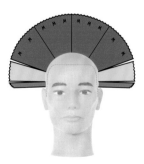

Combination forms consist of two or more of the four basic forms. Careful planning of the proportional relationship of one form to another will allow you to position weight, create expansion and add textural qualities within the form.

LESSONS LEARNED

» The characteristics that each of the four basic forms adds to the combination forms include:

- Solid forms add weight when positioned in the exterior, creating a rectangular shape

- Graduated forms create expansion and an angular shape

- Increase-layered forms elongate the overall form and create an oval shape

- Uniform layers in the interior add volume and create a rounded shape

» When determining the proportional relationship of two or more forms, consider the overall shape, the placement of weight and surface texture desired.

COMBINATION FORM
UNIFORM/GRADUATED

EXPLORE

Why would a client want to combine two different forms into one haircut?

INSPIRE

By changing the proportions, this sculpture can suit a variety of clients and hair textures.

ACHIEVE

Following this *Combination Form – Uniform/Graduated Workshop*, you'll be able to:

>> Create a uniform/graduated combination form hair sculpture incorporating notching and peeling techniques

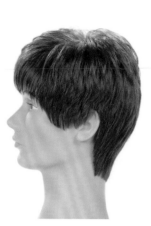

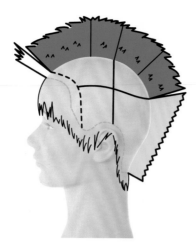

A chunky end texture is achieved by notching high graduation in the exterior. Soft, irregular texture is created by razor peeling uniform lengths in the interior.

Uniform lengths in the interior blend to high graduation in the exterior.

The interior is divided from the exterior, slightly above the upper crest. Each area is sectioned with a center part, from the front, hairline to the nape, and from the apex to each ear. Vertical partings are used in the exterior, and horizontal and pivotal partings are used in the interior. The front hairline is isolated.

7 SCULPTING PROCEDURES

	GRADUATION (EXTERIOR)	GRADUATION (INTERIOR)	UNIFORM

1. SECTION:
Interior from exterior │ Center-front hairline to nape │ Ear to ear

2. HEAD POSITION: Upright

3. PART:
Vertical │ Horizontal │ Pivotal

4. DISTRIBUTE:
Directional (Diagonal) │ Perpendicular

5. PROJECT: High │ 90°

6. FINGER/SHEAR POSITION:
Nonparallel │ parallel

7. DESIGN LINE: Mobile; stationary

COMBINATION FORM UNIFORM/GRADUATED

Draw or fill in the boxes with the appropriate answers.

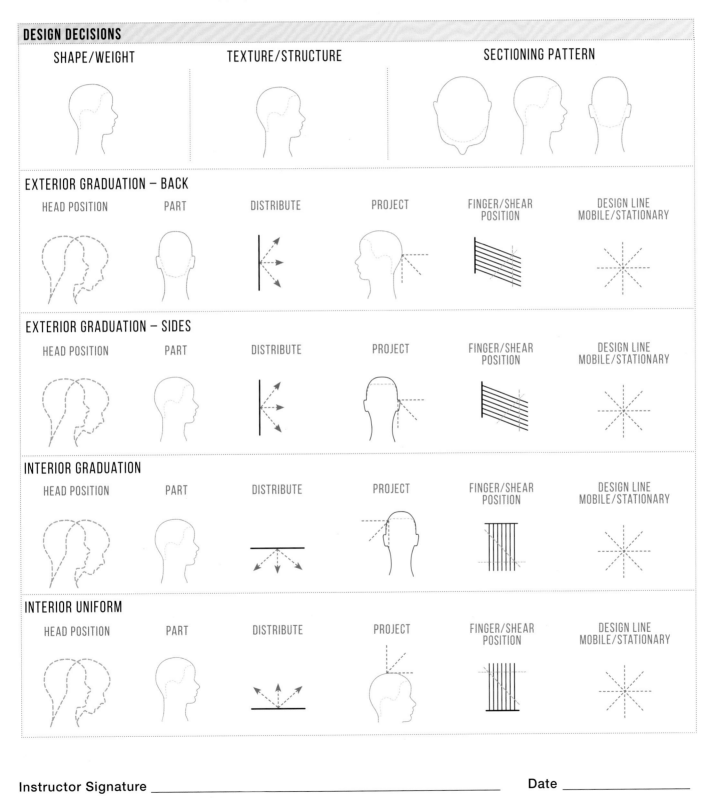

Instructor Signature _____ **Date** _____

PERFORMANCE GUIDE

COMBINATION FORM UNIFORM/GRADUATED

View the video, complete the Design Decisions chart, then perform this workshop. Complete the self-check as you progress through the workshop.

20 mins
Suggested
Salon Speed

PREPARATION	✔

>> Assemble tools and products
>> Set up workstation

☐

SECTIONING AND HEAD POSITION

1. **Section hair:**
   >> Interior from exterior with horseshoe-shaped section
   >> Subsection exterior vertically at each ear

☐

2. **Position head upright.**

☐

EXTERIOR BACK – GRADUATION

3. **Sculpt back using notching technique:**
   >> Vertical partings
   >> Directional distribution (diagonally downward)
   >> High projection
   >> Position fingers nonparallel for high line of inclination
   >> Mobile design line
   >> Sculpt from center to one side until you reach ear

☐

4. **Repeat on opposite side.**

☐

EXTERIOR SIDES – GRADUATION

5. **Sculpt sides using parting behind ear as length guide:**
   >> Vertical partings
   >> Directional distribution
   >> Nonparallel finger position
   >> Mobile design line
   >> Sculpt toward front hairline using notching technique

☐

6. **Sculpt front hairline:**
   - » Vertical parting
   - » Directional distribution
   - » Shift hairline parting back to previously sculpted parting for a subtle length increase
   - » Nonparallel finger position

7. **Repeat on opposite side and check for symmetry.**

INTERIOR – GRADUATION

8. **Sculpt a stationary design line by projecting top lengths of exterior straight out and notching any lengths that protrude.**

   This section will serve as a stationary design line for the interior graduation and to establish a weight area.

9. **Section interior with a center part.**

10. **Sculpt graduation using notching technique:**
    - » Part hair parallel to exterior sectioning line
    - » Distribute lengths to stationary design line
    - » Work from front hairline to center back

11. **Continue using same techniques, working up to center part.**

12. **Repeat same procedures on opposite side:**
    - » Check for symmetry

INTERIOR UNIFORM

13. **Isolate a parting at front hairline to personalize after sculpting uniform lengths.**

14. **Sculpt center uniform length guide:**
    - » Use exterior as length guide
    - » Perpendicular distribution
    - » 90° projection
    - » Fingers parallel to curve of head
    - » Razor-peeling technique
    - » Sculpt from back to front

INTERIOR UNIFORM ✔

15. Sculpt uniform lengths in crown:

>> Pivotal partings
>> 90° projection
>> Parallel finger position
>> Mobile design line
>> Razor-peeling technique
>> Sculpt from center toward side

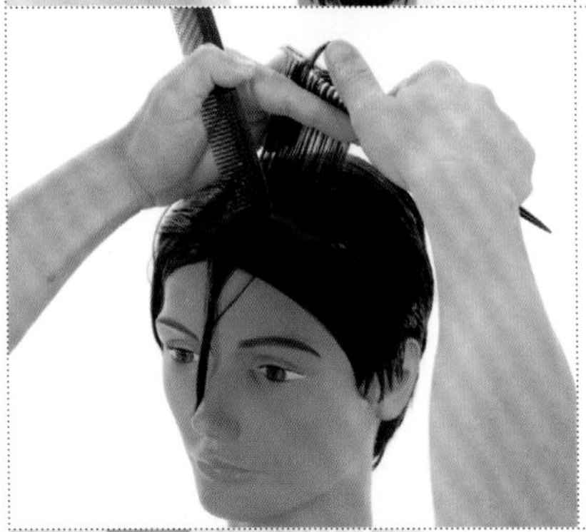

16. Sculpt interior from side to front of section:

>> Horizontal partings
>> 90° projection
>> Mobile design line
>> Razor-peeling technique

17. Sculpt uniform lengths from center back to front on opposite side using same procedures.

PERSONALIZE AND TEXTURIZE

18. Personalize front hairline and perimeter:

>> Razor-etching technique

19. Texturize interior using taper shears:

>> Lift midstrand and ends with comb
>> Close tips of taper shears at midstrand
>> Work from underneath hairstrand

20. The finished sculpture shows soft, activated texture with a fuller, rounded shape in the interior, and more tapered lengths in the exterior.

□

COMPLETION

>> Discard single-use supplies
>> Disinfect tools and multi-use supplies
>> Disinfect workstation and arrange in proper order

□

20 mins
Suggested
Salon Speed

My Speed
_____
_____
_____

INSTRUCTIONS

Record your time in comparison with the suggested salon speed. Then, list here how you could improve your performance.

_____

_____

_____

_____

_____

VARIATION – ASYMMETRIC DISCONNECTED FRINGE

A variation on the combination form – uniform/graduated using notching and peeling techiques to create an asymmetric, disconnected fringe is available online.

➤➤ 105ᶜ GLOSSARY/INDEX

Fringe *45*
Area in front of the apex, which may extend to the outer corner of each eye.

Gel *38*
Creates wet-look finishes.

Gradation *18*
Very short version of the graduated form; shorter exterior lengths gradually progress to longer interior lengths; color-coded yellow; examples include fades and bald fades.

Graduated Form *13*
Consists of shorter exterior lengths that gradually progress toward longer interior lengths; ends appear to stack up along one another at an angle; results in activated texture in the exterior and unactivated in the interior; triangle shape; color-coded yellow; also known as a wedge or 45° angle cut.

Growth Pattern *52*
Determined by the angle and direction at which the hair grows out of the scalp; types include widow's peak, cowlick and whorl.

Hair Sculpting *4*
Artistic carving or removing of hair lengths to create various forms and shapes; also known as haircutting.

Head Position *46*
Position of the client's head during the sculpting process; includes upright, forward or tilted to either side.

High Projection *49, 123*
Refers to holding the hair between 60° and 90° from the curve of the head prior to and while sculpting.

Increase-Layered Form *14*
Consists of shorter interior lengths that progress toward longer exterior lengths; results in a totally activated surface texture with no visible weight; oval shape; color-coded red; also known as a shag or 180° angle cut.

Interior *9, 45*
Area of the head above the crest area.

Line of Inclination *123*
Angle at which the graduation progresses in length; three basic types—low, medium and high.

Low Projection *123*
Refers to holding the hair between 0° to 30° from the curve of the head prior to and while sculpting.

Medium Projection *123*
Refers to holding the hair between 30° and 60° from the curve of the head prior to and while sculpting.

Midstrand Texturizing *207*
Performed between the base area and up to 1" (2.5 cm) before the ends to reduce bulk and weight.

Mobile Design Line *50*
Movable guide that consists of a small amount of previously sculpted hair; used as a length guide to sculpt subsequent partings; also called a traveling guide.

Mousse *38*
A product used to define texture; creates light-to-firm hold on wet or dry hair.

Multiple Design Lines *149*
Two or more stationary design lines used with a conversion layering technique to achieve increase-layered texture; used when lengths do not reach a single stationary design line.

Nape *45*
Area at the back of the head below the occipital bone.

Natural Distribution *48*
Direction the hair assumes as it falls naturally from the head due to gravity.

Natural Fall *49*
Describes the hair as the lengths lay or fall over the curves of the head; projection used for solid form.

Neck Strip *65*
Protects client's skin from contact with the cape; replaces towel during the hair sculpting service.

Nonparallel Finger/Shear Position *50*
Fingers are positioned unequally away from the parting while sculpting.

Normal Projection *7*
The way to analyze the structure or length arrangement of a hair sculpture; hair is viewed abstractly as if it were projected at a 90° angle from the various curves of the head.

Notching *208*
Technique used to create irregular lengths, usually for a chunkier texture at the hair ends.

Occipital *45*
Protruding bone right below the crest area.

Palm Down *29*
Shear position used with the palm of the sculpting hand downward; commonly used for sculpting solid form lengths.

Palm to Palm *29*
Shear position with the palm of sculpting hand facing palm of the other hand.

Palm Up *29*
Shear position used with the palm of the sculpting hand upward; commonly used when sculpting along diagonal lines.

Parallel Finger/Shear Position *50*
Fingers are positioned at an equal distance away from the parting while sculpting; also referred to as parallel sculpting.

Partings *47*
Lines that subdivide sections of hair in order to separate, distribute and control the hair while sculpting.

Perimeter *45*
Area all around the hairline.

Perpendicular Distribution *48*
Hair is combed at a 90°, or right angle, from its base parting.

Planar Sculpting *48*
A technique in which the hair is sculpted along horizontal and vertical planes; hair is distributed straight up, straight out or straight back; used to create a square (rectilinear) form.

Point Cutting *208*
Technique where tips of straight shears are inserted into the strands; movement is from fingers toward ends; creates irregular progression of lengths; also known as pointing.

PIVOT POINT

» ACKNOWLEDGMENTS

Pivot Point Fundamentals is designed to provide education to undergraduate students to help prepare them for licensure and an entry-level position in the cosmetology field. An undertaking of this magnitude requires the expertise and cooperation of many people who are experts in their field. Pivot Point takes pride in our internal team of educators who develop cosmetology, esthetics and nails education, along with our print and digital experts, designers, editors, illustrators and video producers. Pivot Point would like to express our many thanks to these talented individuals who have devoted themselves to the business of beauty, lifelong learning and especially for help raising the bar for future professionals in our industry.

EDUCATION DEVELOPMENT | **Janet Fisher** // **Sabine Held-Perez** // **Vasiliki A. Stavrakis**

Markel Artwell
Eileen Dubelbeis
Brian Fallon
Melissa Holmes
Lisa Luppino
Paul Suttles
Amy Gallagher
Lisa Kersting
Jamie Nabielec
Vic Piccolotto
Ericka Thelin
Jane Wegner

EDITORIAL | **Maureen Spurr** // **Wm. Bullion** // **Deidre Glover**

Liz Bagby
Jack Bernin
Lori Chapman

DESIGN & PRODUCTION | **Jennifer Eckstein** // **Rick Russell** // **Danya Shaikh**

Joanna Jakubowicz
Denise Podlin
Annette Baase
Agnieszka Hansen
Kristine Palmer
Tiffany Wu

PROJECT MANAGEMENT | **Jenny Allen** // **Ken Wegrzyn**

DIGITAL DEVELOPMENT | John Bernin
Javed Fouch
Anna Fehr
Matt McCarthy
Marcia Noriega
Corey Passage
Herb Potzus

Pivot Point also wishes to take this opportunity to acknowledge the many contributors and product concept testers who helped make this program possible.

INDUSTRY CONTRIBUTORS

Linda Burmeister
Esthetics

Jeanne Braa Foster,
Dr. Dean Foster
Eyes on Cancer

Mandy Gross
Nails

Andrea D. Kelly, MA, MSW
University of Delaware

Rosanne Kinley
*Infection Control
National Interstate Council*

Lynn Maestro
Cirépil by Perron Rigot, Paris

Andrzej Matracki
*World and European
Men's Champion*

MODERN SALON

Rachel Molepske
*Look Good Feel Better, PBA
CUT IT OUT, PBA*

Peggy Moon
Liaison to Regulatory and Testing

Robert Richards
Fashion Illustrations

Clif St. Germain, Ph.D
Educational Consultant

Andis Company

International Dermal Institute

HairUWear Inc.

Lock & Loaded Men's Grooming

PRODUCT CONCEPT TESTING

Central Carolina
Community College
Millington, North Carolina

Gateway Community Colleges
Phoenix, Arizona

MC College
Edmonton, Alberta

Metro Beauty Academy
Allentown, Pennsylvania

Rowan Cabarrus
Community College
Kannapolis, North Carolina

Sunstate Academy of
Cosmetology and Massage
Ft. Myers, Florida

Summit Salon Academy
Kokomo, Indiana

TONI&GUY Hairdressing Academy
*Costa Mesa, California
Plano, Texas*

Xenon Academy
*Omaha, NE
Grand Island, NE*

LEADERSHIP TEAM

Robert Passage
Chairman and CEO

Robert J. Sieh
*Senior Vice President,
Finance and Operations*

Judy Rambert
Vice President, Education

Kevin Cameron
*Senior Vice President,
Education and Marketing*

R.W. Miller
*Vice President, Domestic Sales
and Field Education*

Jan Laan
*Vice President, International
Business Development*

Katy O'Mahony
Director, Human Resources

In addition, we give special thanks to the North American Regulating agencies whose careful work protects us as well as our clients, enhancing the high quality of our work. These agencies include Occupational Health and Safety Agency (OSHA) and the U.S. Environmental Protection Agency (EPA). *Pivot Point Fundamentals™* promotes use of their policies and procedures.

Pivot Point International would like to express our SPECIAL THANKS to the inspired visual artisans of Creative Commons, without whose talents this book of beauty would not be possible.

FUNDAMENTALS: COSMETOLOGY

PIVOT POINT®

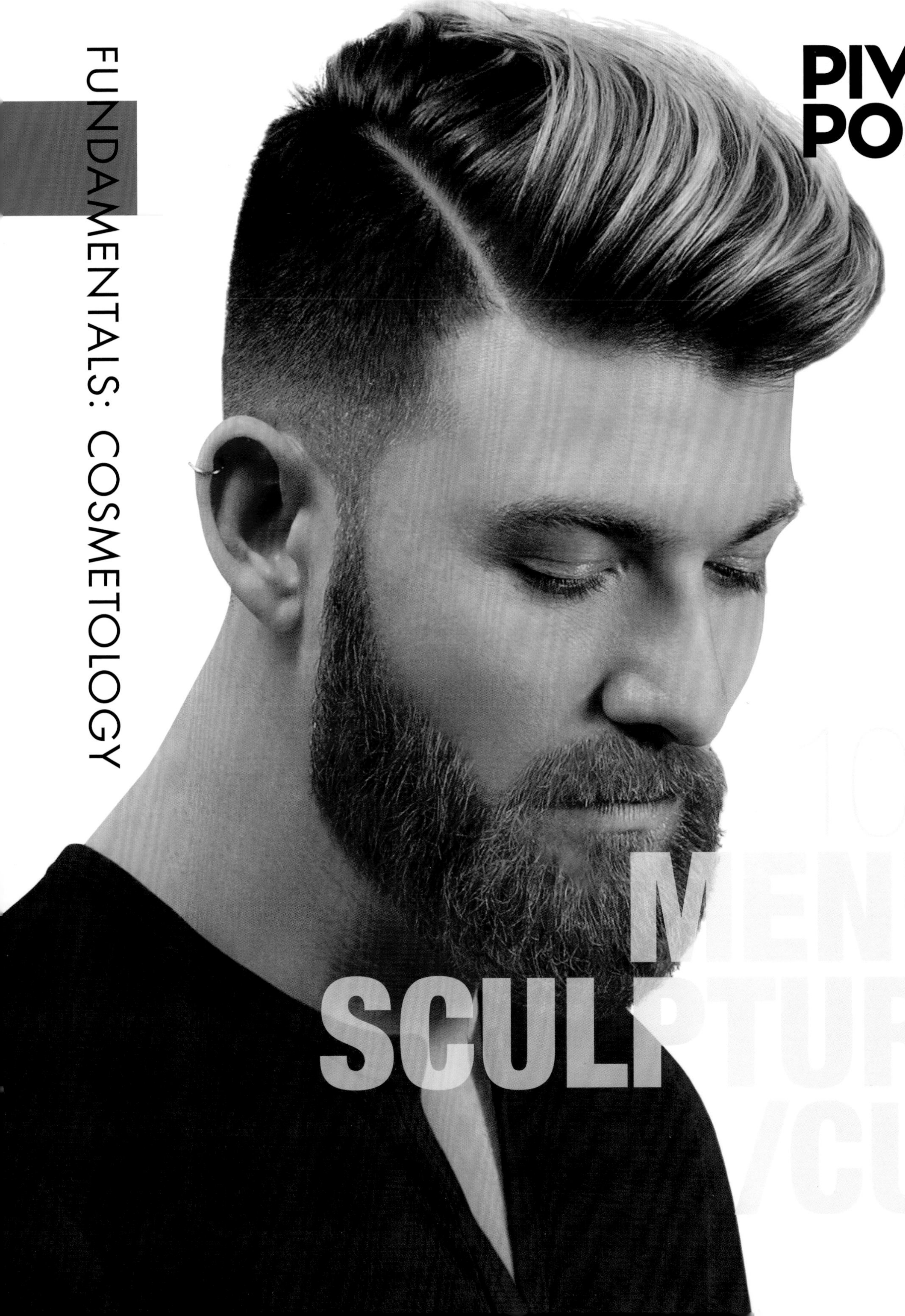

106°

MEN'S SCULPTURE/CUT

ENHANCE YOUR EDUCATION

Augmented Instructions:

Use your mobile device or tablet and any QR-code reader app to scan the target below. This will direct you to the App Store or the Google Play Store to download the Wikitude app, which is used to view our augmented experiences.

When the app is downloaded, find the Wikitude app icon on your device and launch the app.

When opening the Wikitude app for the first time, be sure to allow the app access to the camera on your device.

At the top of the Wikitude app screen, enter "Pivot Point" in the search term window and select "Pivot Point Augmented Experience." The title then appears at the top of your screen.

Now look in the *Pivot Point Fundamentals* books for the icon*. Aim your device so that you see the entire page through your camera. The page will then be augmented so you can view additional content to help you as you work through the lessons.

*Extra augmented content throughout the book is indicated with this icon:

PIVOT POINT

PIVOT POINT FUNDAMENTALS: COSMETOLOGY
MEN'S SCULPTURE/CUT

©1980-2021 Pivot Point International, Inc.
All rights reserved.
ISBN 978-1-940593-44-9

1st Edition
4th Printing, October 2021
Printed in China

Pivot Point International, Inc.
Global Headquarters
8725 West Higgins Road, Suite 700
Chicago, IL 60631 USA

847-866-0500
pivot-point.com

2

CONTENTS
106ᶜ // MEN'S SCULPTURE/CUT

28

2

44

How do the design lines of clothing affect their overall look and feel?

INSPIRE // Learning to recognize the lines of a masculine haircut is the
foundation of a successful men's sculpture.

ACHIEVE // Following this *Men's Sculpture Overview,* you'll be able to:
>> Define planar sculpting
>> Describe overcomb techniques
>> Explain the importance of outlining
>> Identify three facial hair designs

FOCUS // MEN'S SCULPTURE OVERVIEW
Planar Sculpting
Overcomb Techniques
Outlining
Facial Hair Designs

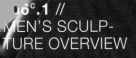

106ᶜ.1 | MEN'S SCULPTURE OVERVIEW

Foundational characteristics of a classic men's haircut include square shapes and clean perimeter hairlines. In this lesson you'll learn about planar sculpting, overcomb techniques and outlining. These techniques along with understanding facial hair options are fundamental skills to build a male clientele.

The **square form** is a combination form, which is created by using the planar sculpting technique.

PLANAR SCULPTING

Planar sculpting is a technique in which the hair is sculpted along imaginary horizontal and vertical planes, independent of the curves of the head. Planar sculpting incorporates directional distribution–distributing the hair straight up, straight out or straight back. A weight area is automatically created where the planes meet, resulting in a square form.

SQUARE FORMS

Pure square forms incorporate planar sculpting throughout the entire haircut. Square form is also referred to as a rectilinear form or a box cut.

Top – Horizontal Partings

The top is sculpted from horizontal partings, distributed straight up and sculpted along a horizontal plane. Fingers and tools are positioned parallel to the floor.

Sides and Back – Horizontal partings

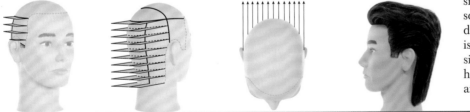

Horizontal partings are used on the sides and back to achieve a strong square silhouette. The sides are distributed straight out, and the back is distributed **straight back**. Both sides and back are sculpted along horizontal planes. Fingers and shears are positioned parallel to the wall.

Sides and Back – Vertical Partings

Vertical partings in the sides and back are another option for planar sculpting. The hair is distributed **straight out**, fingers and shears are positioned perpendicular to the floor, and the hair is sculpted along a vertical plane. The result is a softer square in the back, as seen by comparing these two finishes.

Crown Variation – Strong or Soft Square

The curves and growth patterns at the crown require special consideration when sculpting square forms.

To create a strong square silhouette, distribute crown lengths diagonally upward from vertical partings, sculpt along a vertical plane. This creates longer lengths at the top of the crown.

To soften the square silhouette at the crown, use crown length as a length guide to sculpt the back.

SQUARE FORM COMBINATIONS

Planar sculpting is also used to create a square form in just one area of the head. A popular men's combination is a square interior combined with gradation, a very short form of graduation in the exterior. Square interiors may be blended or disconnected.

Short Square

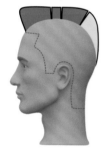

A short square interior, as in this flat top, combined with high gradation is a classic men's sculpture. Shorter lengths tend to stand away from the head and exaggerate the corners of the square interior.

Medium Square

Medium length square interiors are the most versatile since the front can be styled forward or back off the face.

Disconnected

A more edgy version combines a square interior, disconnected from gradation in the exterior. Texturizing creates the illusion of blended lengths.

Reducing Weight Corners

Weight can be reduced or totally removed by rounding the corners of a square interior. Project the hair at 90°, position your fingers parallel to the head, and sculpt to create a more rounded form line.

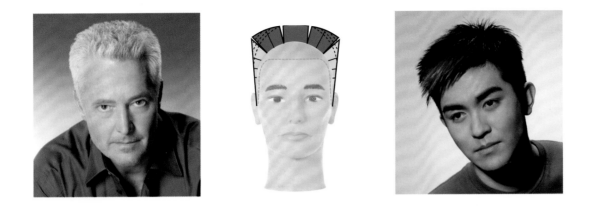

PLANAR SCULPTING GUIDELINES

›› Maintain an upright head position; if the head is tilted, it becomes difficult to judge partings, distribution and finger position.

›› Use the mirror to confirm if you are maintaining directional distribution: straight up, straight out and straight back.

›› Check your fingers periodically to make sure they are positioned horizontally or vertically.

OVERCOMB TECHNIQUES

Overcomb techniques rely on a comb to hold lengths while the hair extending beyond the comb is sculpted with shears, taper shears or clippers. Overcomb techniques are used when hair lengths are too short to hold between your fingers.

COMB CONTROL

Various comb sizes can be used to control the hair while sculpting. The choice of comb varies according to the specific area of the head and the type of overcomb work you are performing.

Large Comb

A large comb is used to quickly remove lengths within larger areas.

Cutting Comb

A cutting comb is used to control shorter lengths.

Taper Comb

A taper or barber comb has a thinner spine and allows you to get close to the head and refine perimeter hairlines.

SHEAR-OVER-COMB

When performing the shear-over-comb technique, the shears are opened and closed repeatedly to remove hair extending beyond the comb.

>> Shears are positioned parallel to the comb.

>> The thumb controls the movable blade.

>> The still blade of the shears should rest gently against the teeth of the comb.

>> Both the shears and comb should move upward in unison.

>> Repeat the technique over the area as many times as necessary to create a smooth progression.

Taper combs allow you to get close to the head and refine perimeter hairlines.

CLIPPER-OVER-COMB

During the clipper-over-comb technique the comb holds the hair while the lengths extending beyond the comb are removed.

>> Clippers are positioned on top of the comb and moved across the comb vertically, horizontally or diagonally.

>> Large combs help you control large areas and create very short square forms such as the flat top.

When working with the taper comb use trimmers because their smaller size helps get into tight spaces.

TAPER-SHEAR-OVER-COMB

Taper shears are used with the overcomb technique to reduce density and increase blending.

Some hair textures, such as fine, straight hair, benefit from additional blending achieved with the taper shears.

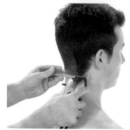

SALON**CONNECTION**

Crossing the Finish Line

Keep your client's comfort in mind and remove hairs off his neck. Talcum powder and neck brushes are commonly used. Some professionals even use a lint roller to remove hair from the skin as well as the collar. A quick rinse at the shampoo bowl is also appreciated.

GRADATION

Gradation is a very short form of graduation achieved with overcomb techniques. Gradation is also known as tapering.

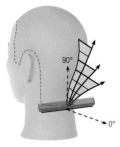

The angle the comb is held controls the resulting length progression and line of inclination. The higher the angle, the closer the comb travels to the head and the shorter the resulting length. There are three types of gradation: low, medium and high.

Transparency
When very short lengths stand out from the head they expose the scalp and create transparency, or the illusion of a lighter hair color. It is important for you to develop an eye for a smooth color progression. Uneven color will identify uneven lengths within the gradation and show you where to re-sculpt to improve the length progression. The higher the angle of the comb, the shorter the hair, and the greater the amount of transparency.

Low Gradation

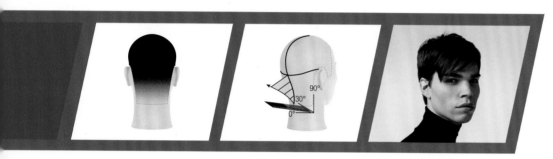

>> Creates the least amount of transparency

>> Line of inclination quickly moves away from the head

>> Shorter lengths located just above the perimeter hairline and below the occipital

Medium Gradation

>> Creates medium transparency

>> The line of inclination moves closer to the head as the amount of gradation increases

>> Extends into the occipital

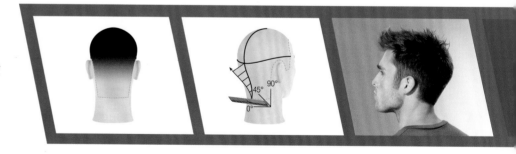

High Gradation

>> Creates maximum transparency

>> The line of inclination is very close to the head

>> Extends above the occipital into the interior

Fade

A fade is an ultra short version of gradation with a high degree of transparency. The name comes from the fact that the hair appears to "fade away" as you approach the perimeter.

» Some areas of the head may be sculpted to the skin, resulting in a **"bald fade."**

» This type of sculpture is almost always done with clippers and requires careful blending.

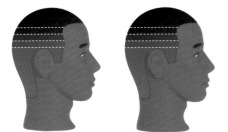

Zones, which define a progression of lengths and the amount of transparency, should be predetermined so that the design is well-balanced. The lowest zone in the design is sculpted the shortest while lengths gradually get longer in zones toward the interior.

» Blend the zones to create smooth transitions.

» Blending may be achieved freehand by arcing the clippers away from the head, or by using a progression of attachments or guards.

OVERCOMB GUIDELINES

Ensure predictable results by following the overcomb guidelines below.

» Keep client's head position consistent while using overcomb techniques.

» Only move the thumb of your sculpting hand during the shear-over-comb technique. The still blade of the shears should rest gently against the teeth of the comb, and both tools should travel in unison.

» Change the sculpting direction and sculpt against the "grain" of the hair, against the growth pattern. This helps ensure that all the hair is picked up and controlled by the comb.

» Choose taper-shear-over-comb technique in higher density areas to achieve even transparency.

OUTLINING

Outlining is a sculpting technique used to define the perimeter hairline. Attention to the perimeter, and how it is defined or lined, is an important final step in men's haircutting. In general, follow the natural hairline. The tips of the shears are often used first to outline the entire hairline, including the sideburns, around the ears and along the nape. Carefully work around the ears. Bend the ear slightly forward to outline behind the ears and slightly back to outline in front of the ears.

Clippers or trimmers can be used to sculpt the hair beyond the outlined area. The clipper or trimmer blades are placed against the skin and the hair is sculpted section by section.

ALERT!

Use extreme caution when sculpting on the skin with the razor. Cosmetologists may not be allowed to perform this service. Be guided by your regulatory agency.

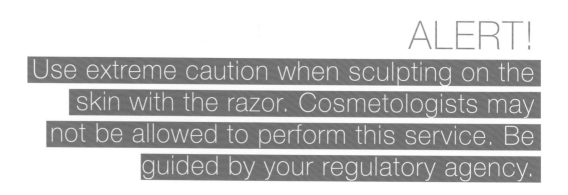

HAIR TATTOOS

Hair tattoos are creative outlines carved into the hair. These special designs are also called graphics, and range from a carved part to complex patterns with straight and curved lines. Tattoo designs and carved parts can be created with trimmers and/or a razor. Make sure you know how daring your client is and gain approval before you begin carving. Also, since hair grows quickly, clients need to be aware that frequent appointments are required to keep a hair tattoo or carved part fresh.

FACIAL HAIR DESIGNS

Designing facial hair—beards, goatees, mustaches, and sideburns—is a special service you can offer your male clients. Facial hair can be worn as a fashion statement or to enhance or balance facial features. The popularity of facial hair is influenced by current trends and individual lifestyle.

Facial hair also includes unwanted hair that requires grooming, such as unruly eyebrows and excess hair on the ears. Adding a few grooming steps to the end of a haircut takes only a few minutes, and can make a big difference to your client's final appearance.

Eyebrows	Earlobes	Inside of Ears
		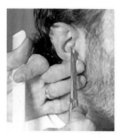
Comb the hair upward and trim the hair that extends beyond the comb.	Hold his earlobe and carefully use the tips of shears—or the trimmers—to trim extra hairs.	Trim excess hair within the ear with tips of the shears. Balance the shears with your fingers for additional control.

Beard trims may be offered in your salon depending on your regulatory guidelines. Outlining, overcomb and freeform techniques are used to establish the shape desired.

Use clippers on larger areas. Position blade against the skin.	Use trimmers on tighter areas.	Work to create symmetry.
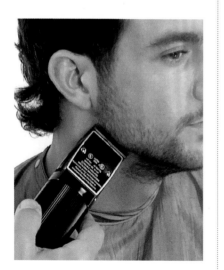	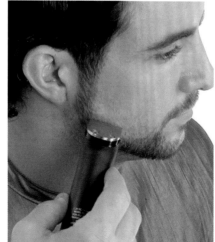	

FACIAL HAIR

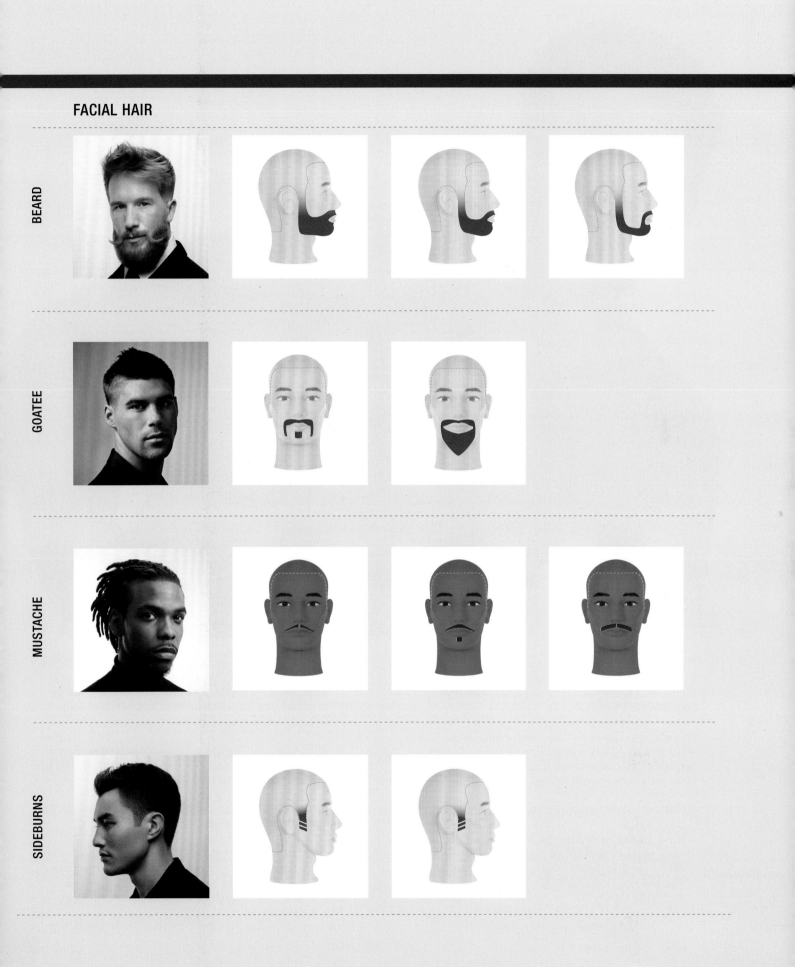

BEARD

GOATEE

MUSTACHE

SIDEBURNS

LESSONS LEARNED

>> Planar Sculpting: Sculpting along imaginary horizontal and vertical planes independent of the curves of the head. The planar sculpting technique is used to create square forms.

>> Overcomb techniques: The comb controls the hair when it is too short to hold between your fingers. Includes shear-over-comb, clipper-over-comb and taper-shear-over-comb techniques.

>> Gradation: Very short progression of hair length.

   ▪ Low gradation creates the least amount of transparency positioned just above the perimeter. The line of inclination quickly moves away from the head.

   ▪ Medium gradation creates a medium degree of transparency from the perimeter and extends into the occipital. The line of inclination moves closer to the head as the amount of gradation increases.

   ▪ High gradation creates maximum transparency from the perimeter and extends above the occipital. The line of inclination moves very close to the head.

>> Outlining: Clean lines around the hairline and sideburns. Tools used for outlining are shears, clippers and trimmers.

>> Facial Hair: The main categories of facial hair are beards, goatees, mustaches, and sideburns. Additional grooming– such as removing stray hairs from the eyebrows and on the ears–is an appreciated finishing touch to a men's hair sculpture.

SQUARE FORM

EXPLORE

How do you think designers achieve short-layered sculptures that have the appearance of a square shape?

INSPIRE

Learning how to sculpt along a plane will enable you to cater to a male clientele who desires a strong, masculine appearance!

ACHIEVE

Following this *Square Form Workshop*, you'll be able to:

>> Create a square form hair sculpture using the planar sculpting technique

>> Create mobility within the form using taper shears

>> Air form the square form using finger-styling techniques

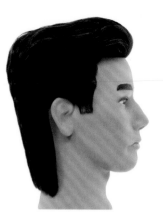

The square form is a classic, masculine shape that can be adapted and styled to suit a variety of looks desired by the male clientele.

The square form is a combination of increase, uniform and graduated forms. This combination form is automatically created using the planar sculpting technique. The perimeter hairline is refined for additional perimeter weight.

A horseshoe-shaped section is used to subdivide the interior from the exterior. The top and back each include 3 panels that are sculpted from horizontal partings. The sides are sculpted from horizontal partings. Vertical partings are used in the crown to blend the back with the top. The planar sculpting technique is used throughout.

7 SCULPTING PROCEDURES

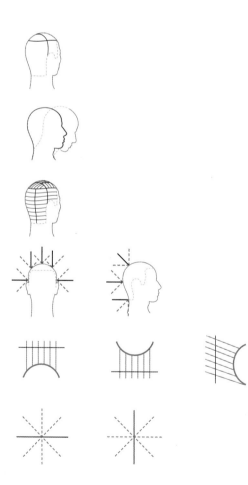

1. SECTION:
   (2) Interior/exterior horseshoe-shaped section

2. HEAD POSITION: Upright

3. PART:
   Top, back, sides: Horizontal | Crown: Vertical

4-5. DISTRIBUTE/PROJECT:
   | Top: | Straight up | Sides: | Straight out |
   | Back: | Straight back | Crown: | Diagonal upward |

6. FINGER/SHEAR POSITION:
   Top: Horizontal (parallel to floor)
   Back and Sides: Horizontal (parallel to wall)
   Crown: Vertical (perpendicular to floor)

7. DESIGN LINE:
   Top, back and sides: Horizontal | Crown: Vertical

SQUARE FORM

Draw or fill in the boxes with the appropriate answers.

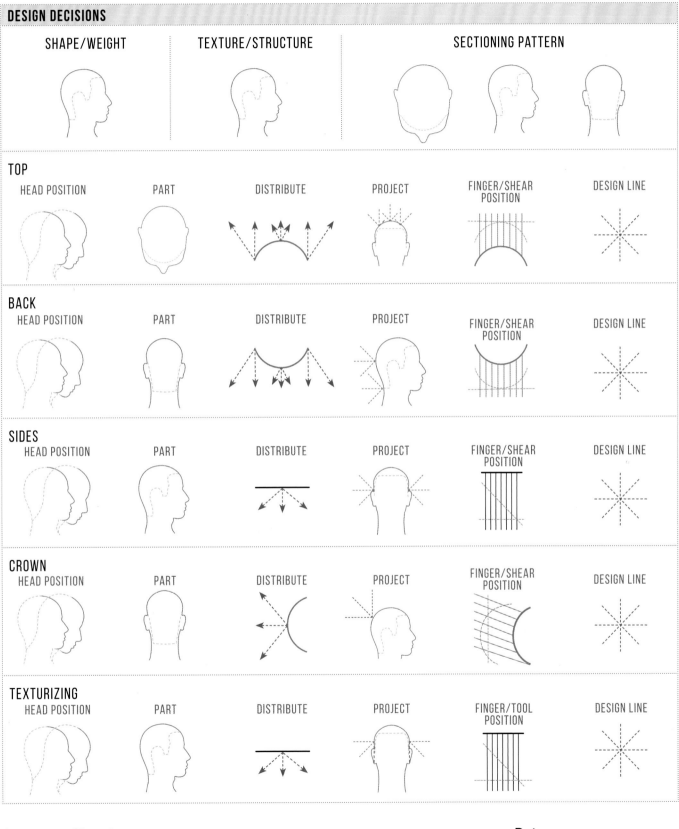

DESIGN DECISIONS

| SHAPE/WEIGHT | TEXTURE/STRUCTURE | SECTIONING PATTERN | | |

TOP

| HEAD POSITION | PART | DISTRIBUTE | PROJECT | FINGER/SHEAR POSITION | DESIGN LINE |

BACK

| HEAD POSITION | PART | DISTRIBUTE | PROJECT | FINGER/SHEAR POSITION | DESIGN LINE |

SIDES

| HEAD POSITION | PART | DISTRIBUTE | PROJECT | FINGER/SHEAR POSITION | DESIGN LINE |

CROWN

| HEAD POSITION | PART | DISTRIBUTE | PROJECT | FINGER/SHEAR POSITION | DESIGN LINE |

TEXTURIZING

| HEAD POSITION | PART | DISTRIBUTE | PROJECT | FINGER/TOOL POSITION | DESIGN LINE |

Instructor Signature _____   **Date** _____

PERFORMANCE GUIDE

SQUARE FORM

View the video, complete the Design Decisions chart, then perform this workshop. Complete the self-check as you progress through the workshop.

30 mins
Suggested
Salon Speed

PREPARATION	✔
>> Assemble tools and products >> Set up workstation	☐

SECTIONING – HEAD POSITION – LENGTH GUIDE

1. Section interior from exterior:
>> Extend horizontal parting from recession area to center back
>> Subdivide exterior with a vertical parting from horizontal parting to just behind ear
>> Subdivide interior by extending vertical parting to top, slightly behind apex
>> Repeat on opposite side
>> Clip and isolate crown lengths for control

☐

2. Sculpt length guide at bridge of nose:
>> Release a thin vertical center panel at top
>> Distribute panel in natural fall; avoid projection
>> Sculpt horizontally at bridge of nose

☐

3. Position head upright.

☐

4. Sculpt center panel to establish interior length guide:
>> Distribute hair straight up
>> Position fingers horizontally
>> Sculpt parallel to floor, following initial length guide at front hairline
>> Sculpt from front to apex

☐

5. **Subdivide top into 3 equal panels:**

    Note: Each panel is sculpted from horizontal partings.

6. **Planar sculpting technique is used to sculpt each panel:**
    >> Each horizontal parting is distributed straight up and sculpted horizontally
    >> Each panel is sculpted from the back (apex) to front hairline
    >> The planar sculpting technique automatically creates uniform layers and a length increase toward front and back

7. **Begin to sculpt Panel 1 using planar sculpting technique:**
    >> Distribute hair straight up from horizontal parting
    >> Position fingers horizontally (parallel to floor)
    >> Sculpt parallel to fingers, following center length guide
    >> Work from back of panel to front hairline

8. **Complete Panel 1 using planar sculpting technique:**
    >> Keep hair evenly moist throughout sculpture

9. **Sculpt Panel 2 using planar sculpting technique:**
    >> Work from back of panel to front hairline
    >> Use a portion of Panel 1 as length guide
    >> Distribute hair straight up from horizontal partings
    >> Position fingers horizontally (parallel to floor)
    >> Sculpt parallel to floor

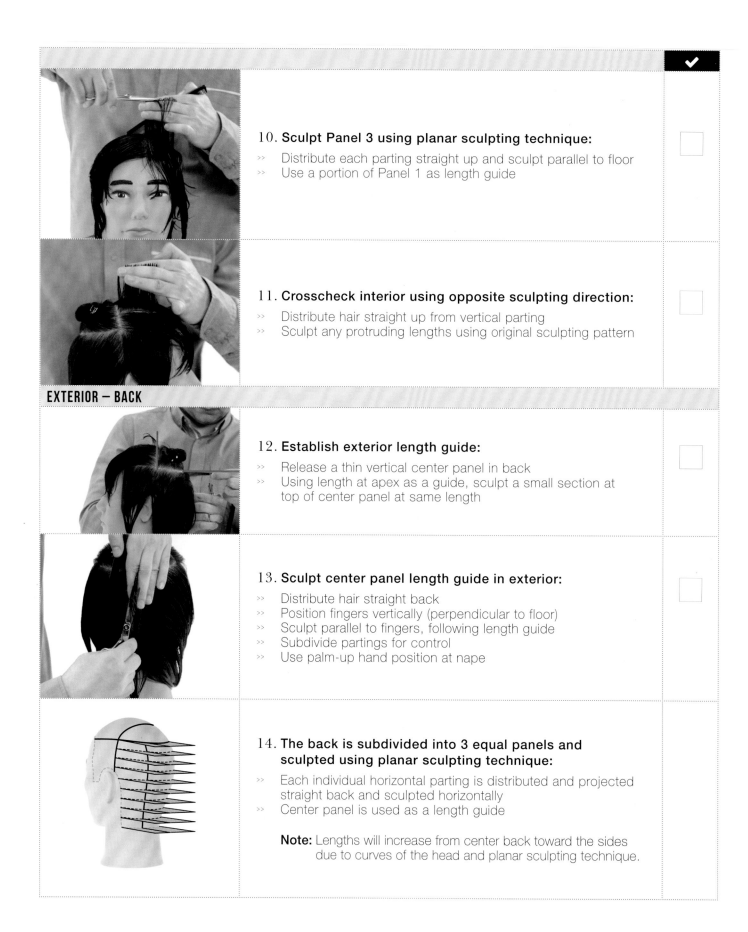

10. **Sculpt Panel 3 using planar sculpting technique:**
   >> Distribute each parting straight up and sculpt parallel to floor
   >> Use a portion of Panel 1 as length guide

11. **Crosscheck interior using opposite sculpting direction:**
   >> Distribute hair straight up from vertical parting
   >> Sculpt any protruding lengths using original sculpting pattern

EXTERIOR – BACK

12. **Establish exterior length guide:**
   >> Release a thin vertical center panel in back
   >> Using length at apex as a guide, sculpt a small section at top of center panel at same length

13. **Sculpt center panel length guide in exterior:**
   >> Distribute hair straight back
   >> Position fingers vertically (perpendicular to floor)
   >> Sculpt parallel to fingers, following length guide
   >> Subdivide partings for control
   >> Use palm-up hand position at nape

14. **The back is subdivided into 3 equal panels and sculpted using planar sculpting technique:**
   >> Each individual horizontal parting is distributed and projected straight back and sculpted horizontally
   >> Center panel is used as a length guide

   Note: Lengths will increase from center back toward the sides due to curves of the head and planar sculpting technique.

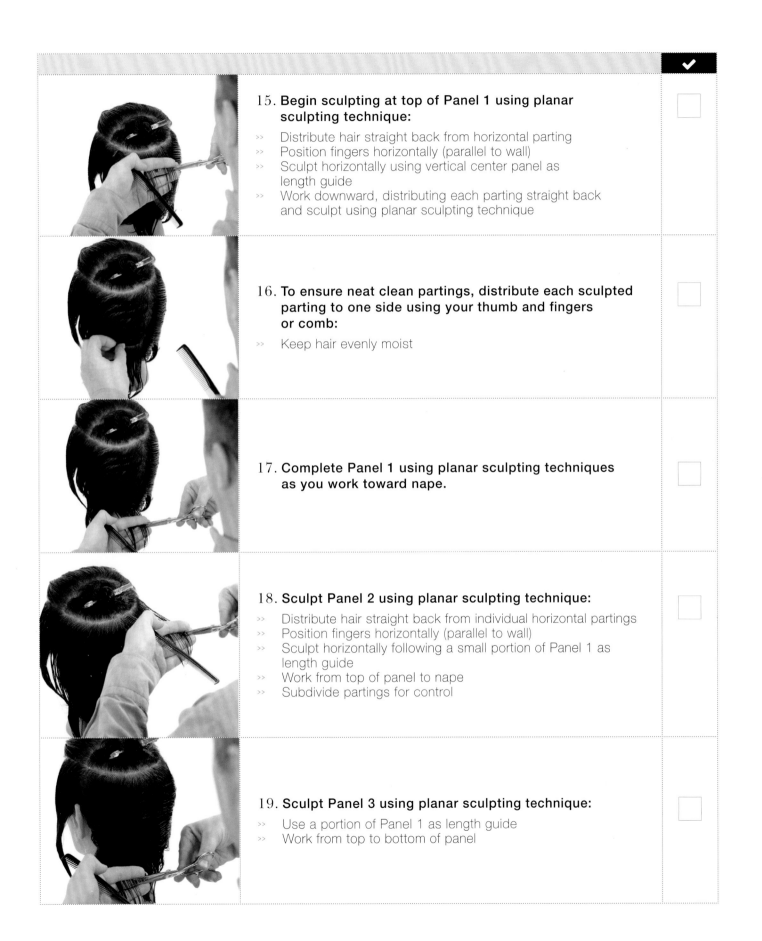

15. **Begin sculpting at top of Panel 1 using planar sculpting technique:**
>> Distribute hair straight back from horizontal parting
>> Position fingers horizontally (parallel to wall)
>> Sculpt horizontally using vertical center panel as length guide
>> Work downward, distributing each parting straight back and sculpt using planar sculpting technique

16. **To ensure neat clean partings, distribute each sculpted parting to one side using your thumb and fingers or comb:**
>> Keep hair evenly moist

17. **Complete Panel 1 using planar sculpting techniques as you work toward nape.**

18. **Sculpt Panel 2 using planar sculpting technique:**
>> Distribute hair straight back from individual horizontal partings
>> Position fingers horizontally (parallel to wall)
>> Sculpt horizontally following a small portion of Panel 1 as length guide
>> Work from top of panel to nape
>> Subdivide partings for control

19. **Sculpt Panel 3 using planar sculpting technique:**
>> Use a portion of Panel 1 as length guide
>> Work from top to bottom of panel

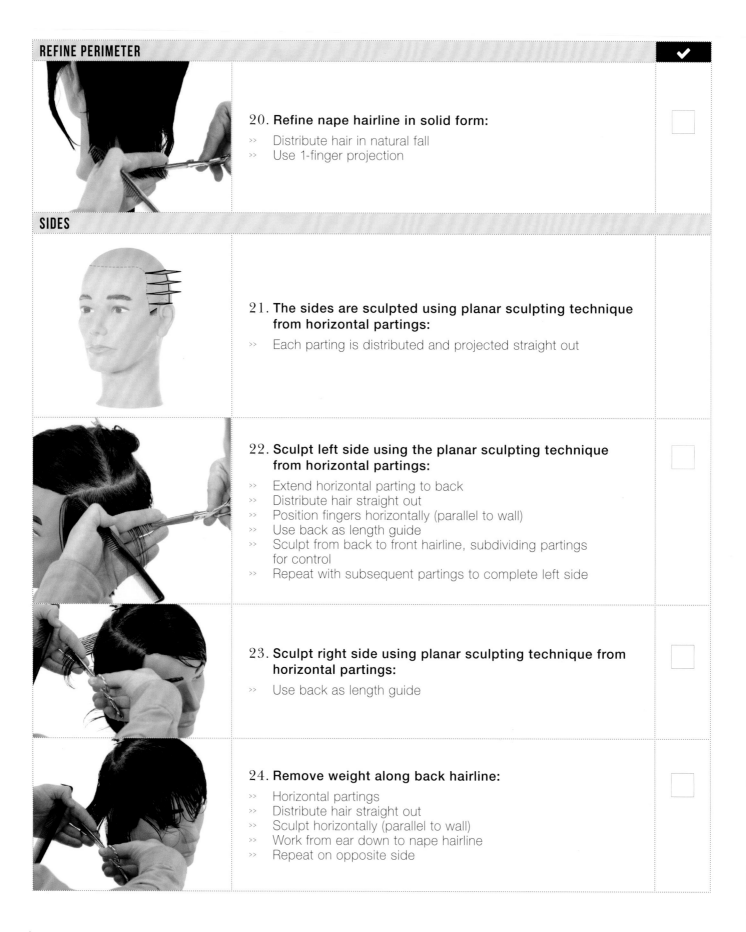

REFINE PERIMETER ✔

20. **Refine nape hairline in solid form:**

>> Distribute hair in natural fall
>> Use 1-finger projection

SIDES

21. **The sides are sculpted using planar sculpting technique from horizontal partings:**

>> Each parting is distributed and projected straight out

22. **Sculpt left side using the planar sculpting technique from horizontal partings:**

>> Extend horizontal parting to back
>> Distribute hair straight out
>> Position fingers horizontally (parallel to wall)
>> Use back as length guide
>> Sculpt from back to front hairline, subdividing partings for control
>> Repeat with subsequent partings to complete left side

23. **Sculpt right side using planar sculpting technique from horizontal partings:**

>> Use back as length guide

24. **Remove weight along back hairline:**

>> Horizontal partings
>> Distribute hair straight out
>> Sculpt horizontally (parallel to wall)
>> Work from ear down to nape hairline
>> Repeat on opposite side

25. **The crown is sculpted from vertical partings and multiple stationary design lines:**

>> Each parting is distributed diagonally upward
>> Each parting is sculpted vertically to maintain weight and length at crown
>> Each parting is distributed to previously sculpted parting

26. **Sculpt crown using the shortest point from exterior:**

>> Release a vertical parting in center
>> Distribute hair diagonally upward
>> Position fingers perpendicular to floor
>> Sculpt parallel to fingers
>> Work from the center to one side until lengths no longer reach
>> Work from center to opposite side using same techniques

27. **Once the crown is sculpted, a length increase automatically occurs from the center to the sides resulting in a concave line. The longer lengths towards the sides creates a weight area in the square form.**

CROWN/TOP AND SIDES

28. **Blend crown and top lengths:**

>> Release a center vertical parting from top (apex) to crown
>> Distribute hair straight up
>> Position fingers horizontally (parallel to floor)
>> Sculpt to blend crown with top lengths
>> Repeat with subsequent partings until lengths no longer reach
>> Repeat from center to opposite side

29. **Blend top and sides:**

>> Vertical partings
>> Distribute hair straight out
>> Position fingers vertically (perpendicular to floor)
>> Sculpt corner to blend

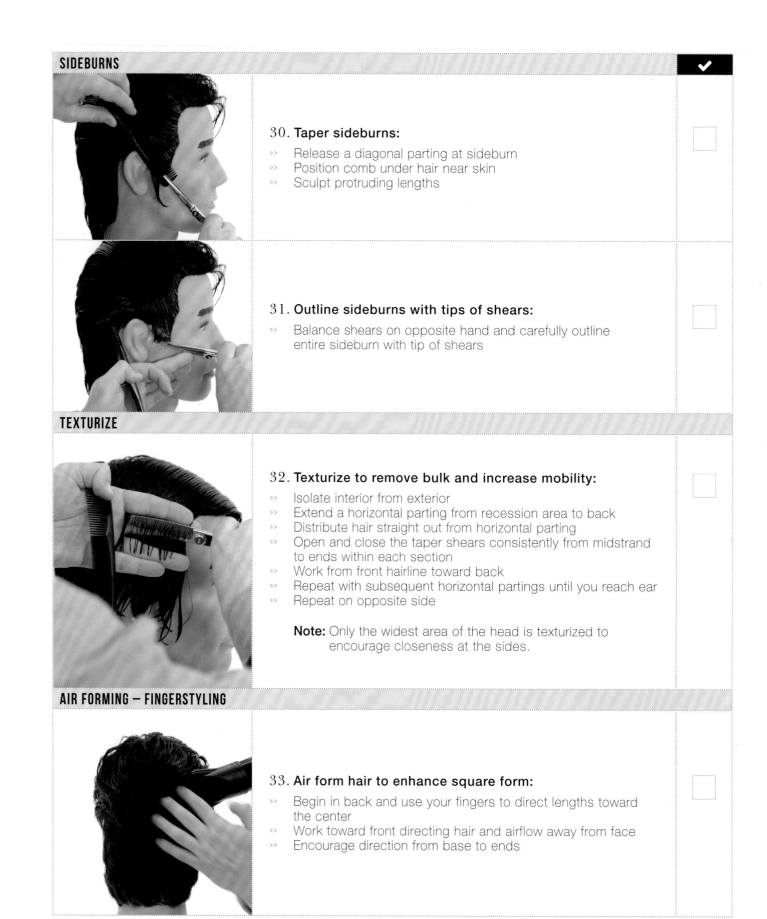

SIDEBURNS ✔

30. **Taper sideburns:**
>> Release a diagonal parting at sideburn
>> Position comb under hair near skin
>> Sculpt protruding lengths

31. **Outline sideburns with tips of shears:**
>> Balance shears on opposite hand and carefully outline entire sideburn with tip of shears

TEXTURIZE

32. **Texturize to remove bulk and increase mobility:**
>> Isolate interior from exterior
>> Extend a horizontal parting from recession area to back
>> Distribute hair straight out from horizontal parting
>> Open and close the taper shears consistently from midstrand to ends within each section
>> Work from front hairline toward back
>> Repeat with subsequent horizontal partings until you reach ear
>> Repeat on opposite side

Note: Only the widest area of the head is texturized to encourage closeness at the sides.

AIR FORMING – FINGERSTYLING

33. **Air form hair to enhance square form:**
>> Begin in back and use your fingers to direct lengths toward the center
>> Work toward front directing hair and airflow away from face
>> Encourage direction from base to ends

34. Apply product and finish:

>> Rub a dime-sized amount of styling gum into your palms
>> Lightly distribute to surface
>> Reinforce direction and shape
>> Use fingertips to create textural interest

35. The finish shows an angular silhouette that is desired by many male clients.

COMPLETION

>> Discard single-use supplies
>> Disinfect tools and multi-use supplies
>> Disinfect workstation and arrange in proper order

30 mins
Suggested
Salon Speed

My Speed
_____
_____
_____

INSTRUCTIONS:

Record your time in comparison with the suggested salon speed. Then, list here how you could improve your performance.

_____

_____

_____

_____

_____

VARIATION – ROUNDED SQUARE FORM – VERTICAL PARTINGS

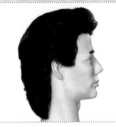

A variation on the square form using vertical partings at the sides and back, along with sculpting a uniform nape, is available online.

HIGH GRADATION
SHEAR-OVER-COMB

EXPLORE

Can you name some animals that have long manes of hair, or birds that have cool hairstyles?

INSPIRE

Disconnected shapes with longer interior lengths are in high demand among male clients.

ACHIEVE

Following this *High Gradation, Shear-Over-Comb Workshop*, you'll be able to:

>> Create high gradation in the exterior using the shear-over-comb technique

>> Texturize with taper shears to blend a shorter exterior with a contrasting longer interior

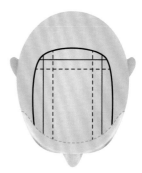

High gradation in the exterior contrasts with the longer interior square form. The longer interior lengths allow for styling versatility.

The shear-over-comb technique is used to sculpt high gradation in the exterior. The previously sculpted square form in the interior is texturized to encourage blending between the two disconnected shapes.

A horseshoe-shaped section is used to subdivide the interior from the exterior. Horizontal partings are used in the interior to texturize the hair.

7 SCULPTING PROCEDURES

EXTERIOR   INTERIOR

1. SECTION:
   Horseshoe-shaped (exterior/interior)

2. HEAD POSITION: Upright

3. PART:
   N/A (exterior) │ Horizontal (interior)

   N/A

4. DISTRIBUTE:
   Perpendicular (exterior)
   Directional-straight back/out (interior)

5. PROJECT:
   90° (exterior) │ Straight back/out (interior)

6. FINGER/SHEAR POSITION: Parallel

7. DESIGN LINE:
   Diagonal/high line of inclination (exterior)
   Horizontal (interior)

DESIGN DECISIONS CHART

HIGH GRADATION SHEAR-OVER-COMB

Draw or fill in the boxes with the appropriate answers.

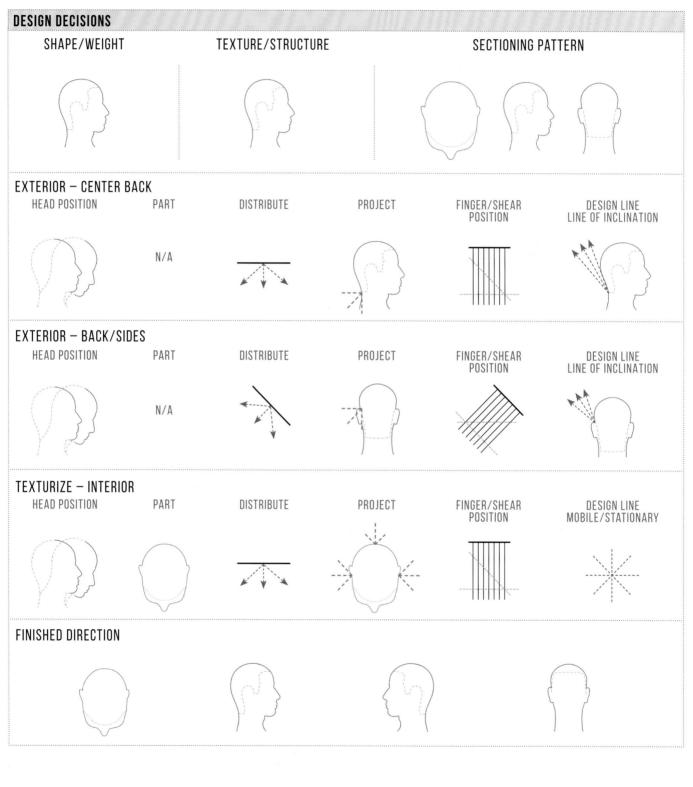

DESIGN DECISIONS

SHAPE/WEIGHT	TEXTURE/STRUCTURE	SECTIONING PATTERN

EXTERIOR – CENTER BACK

HEAD POSITION	PART	DISTRIBUTE	PROJECT	FINGER/SHEAR POSITION	DESIGN LINE LINE OF INCLINATION
	N/A				

EXTERIOR – BACK/SIDES

HEAD POSITION	PART	DISTRIBUTE	PROJECT	FINGER/SHEAR POSITION	DESIGN LINE LINE OF INCLINATION
	N/A				

TEXTURIZE – INTERIOR

HEAD POSITION	PART	DISTRIBUTE	PROJECT	FINGER/SHEAR POSITION	DESIGN LINE MOBILE/STATIONARY

FINISHED DIRECTION

Instructor Signature _____ **Date** _____

HIGH GRADATION
SHEAR-OVER-COMB

View the video, complete the Design Decisions chart, and then perform this workshop. Complete the self-check as you progress through the workshop.

30 mins
Suggested Salon Speed

PREPARATION	✔
>> Assemble tools and products >> Set up workstation	☐

SECTIONING – HEAD POSITION

1. **High gradation is sculpted in the exterior:**
   >> Angle of comb is approximately 65°
   >> Angle of comb and distance between comb and head will control length progression and line of inclination
   >> Closer comb is held to head, the shorter the length and more transparent the results

2. **Section interior from exterior:**
   >> Horseshoe-shaped section using recession area as a guide ☐

EXTERIOR – HIGH GRADATION – SHEAR-OVER-COMB

3. **Position head upright.** ☐

4. **Sculpt high gradation in center back using shear-over-comb technique:** ☐
   >> Project hair at 90°
   >> Control angle of comb with thumb and index finger
   >> Keep still blade of shears parallel to spine of comb
   >> Move comb and shears upward in unison and sculpt protruding lengths
   >> Gradually work up from hairline to interior
   >> Flip comb to redistribute hair as often as necessary

5. **Complete center back using shear-over-comb technique.** ☐

   Note: The width of the panel is determined by the shape of the head and where the back begins to curve toward the side.

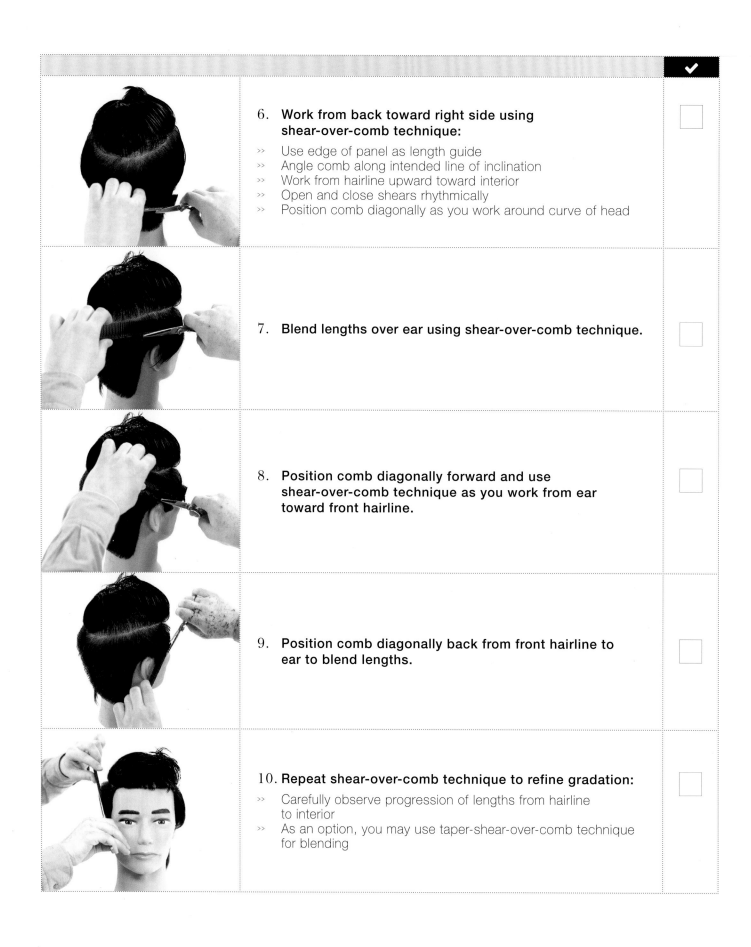

6. **Work from back toward right side using shear-over-comb technique:**

>> Use edge of panel as length guide
>> Angle comb along intended line of inclination
>> Work from hairline upward toward interior
>> Open and close shears rhythmically
>> Position comb diagonally as you work around curve of head

7. **Blend lengths over ear using shear-over-comb technique.**

8. **Position comb diagonally forward and use shear-over-comb technique as you work from ear toward front hairline.**

9. **Position comb diagonally back from front hairline to ear to blend lengths.**

10. **Repeat shear-over-comb technique to refine gradation:**

>> Carefully observe progression of lengths from hairline to interior
>> As an option, you may use taper-shear-over-comb technique for blending

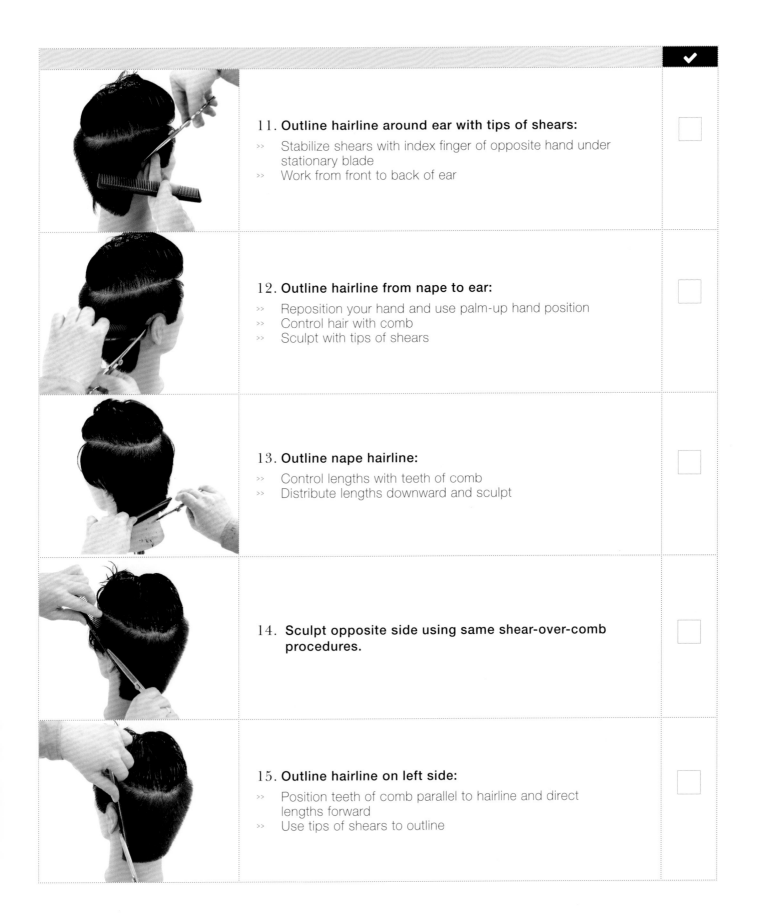

11. Outline hairline around ear with tips of shears:

>> Stabilize shears with index finger of opposite hand under stationary blade

>> Work from front to back of ear

12. Outline hairline from nape to ear:

>> Reposition your hand and use palm-up hand position

>> Control hair with comb

>> Sculpt with tips of shears

13. Outline nape hairline:

>> Control lengths with teeth of comb

>> Distribute lengths downward and sculpt

14. Sculpt opposite side using same shear-over-comb procedures.

15. Outline hairline on left side:

>> Position teeth of comb parallel to hairline and direct lengths forward

>> Use tips of shears to outline

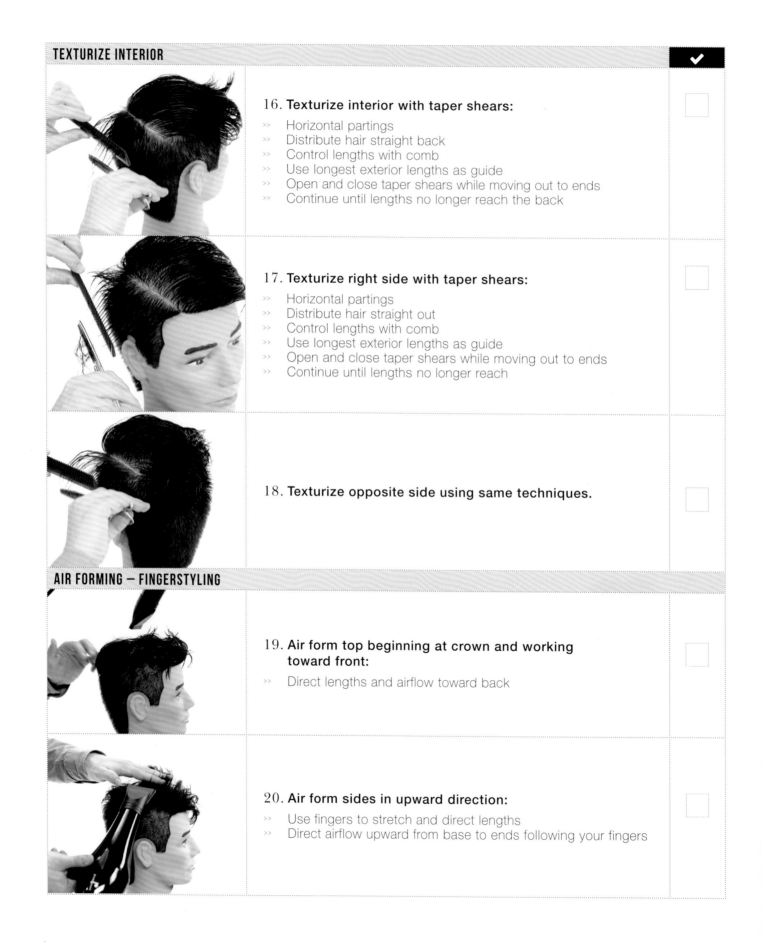

TEXTURIZE INTERIOR ✔

16. Texturize interior with taper shears:
>> Horizontal partings
>> Distribute hair straight back
>> Control lengths with comb
>> Use longest exterior lengths as guide
>> Open and close taper shears while moving out to ends
>> Continue until lengths no longer reach the back

17. Texturize right side with taper shears:
>> Horizontal partings
>> Distribute hair straight out
>> Control lengths with comb
>> Use longest exterior lengths as guide
>> Open and close taper shears while moving out to ends
>> Continue until lengths no longer reach

18. Texturize opposite side using same techniques.

AIR FORMING — FINGERSTYLING

19. Air form top beginning at crown and working toward front:
>> Direct lengths and airflow toward back

20. Air form sides in upward direction:
>> Use fingers to stretch and direct lengths
>> Direct airflow upward from base to ends following your fingers

21. **Use tension with fingers to create maximum volume and textural interest with front lengths.**

22. **Create curvature movement and direction:**
    >> Position fingers at base and rotate your fingers in a circular motion while stretching hair upward
    >> Work from left side to front

23. **Apply a fibrous styling product and finish as desired:**
    >> Separate ends to create textural interest

24. **The finish shows high gradation in the exterior and a longer, disconnected interior well-suited for a variety of male clients.**

COMPLETION

>> Discard single-use supplies
>> Disinfect tools and multi-use supplies
>> Disinfect workstation and arrange in proper order

30 mins
Suggested
Salon Speed

My Speed
_____
_____
_____

INSTRUCTIONS:

Record your time in comparison with the suggested salon speed. To improve my performance, I need to:

_____
_____
_____
_____

HIGH GRADATION
CLIPPER-OVER-COMB

EXPLORE

How would you describe the main characteristics of a box?

INSPIRE

Clean masculine lines, a short, tight perimeter and easy upkeep make this cut a frequently requested classic.

ACHIEVE

Following this *High Gradation, Clipper-Over-Comb Workshop,* you'll be able to:

>> Create a short square form in the interior

>> Demonstrate end tapering with taper shears

>> Create high gradation in the exterior using a clipper-over-comb technique

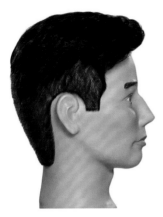

The square interior creates an angular shape. The clippers create a broom-like texture in the exterior.

High gradation in the exterior blends to the square form in the interior. End tapering increases texture in the interior.

The interior is subdivided from the exterior. The interior is further subdivided into three sections and horizontal partings are used.

7 SCULPTING PROCEDURES

1. SECTION:
   Interior (3)/Exterior

2. HEAD POSITION: Upright

3. PART:
   Horizontal (interior)

4. DISTRIBUTE:
   Straight up (interior/directional)

5. PROJECT:
   Straight up (interior) | 90° (exterior)

6. FINGER/SHEAR POSITION:

   Parallel to floor (interior)
   Clippers horizontally across comb (exterior)

7. DESIGN LINE:
   Mobile (interior)

DESIGN DECISIONS CHART

HIGH GRADATION CLIPPER-OVER-COMB

Draw or fill in the boxes with the appropriate answers.

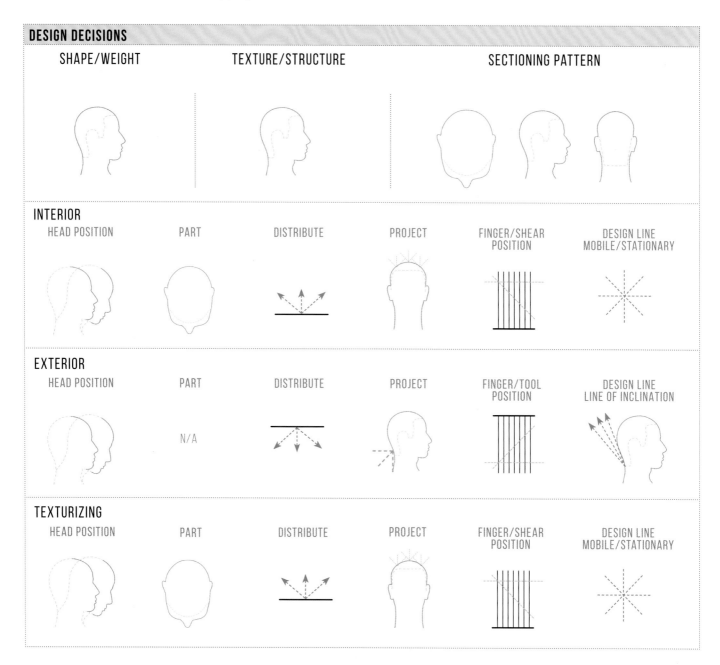

DESIGN DECISIONS		
SHAPE/WEIGHT	TEXTURE/STRUCTURE	SECTIONING PATTERN

INTERIOR

| HEAD POSITION | PART | DISTRIBUTE | PROJECT | FINGER/SHEAR POSITION | DESIGN LINE MOBILE/STATIONARY |

EXTERIOR

| HEAD POSITION | PART | DISTRIBUTE | PROJECT | FINGER/TOOL POSITION | DESIGN LINE LINE OF INCLINATION |
| | N/A | | | | |

TEXTURIZING

| HEAD POSITION | PART | DISTRIBUTE | PROJECT | FINGER/SHEAR POSITION | DESIGN LINE MOBILE/STATIONARY |

Instructor Signature _____ Date _____

HIGH GRADATION
CLIPPER-OVER-COMB

View the video, complete the Design Decisions chart, then perform this workshop. Complete the self-check as you progress through the workshop.

20 mins
Suggested Salon Speed

PREPARATION		✔
	» Assemble tools and products » Set up workstation	☐

SECTION – HEAD POSITION

1. **Section hair into 4 areas:**
   - » Interior from exterior
   - » Divide interior into 3 panels

   ☐

2. **Position head upright.**

   ☐

INTERIOR – SQUARE FORM

3. **Interior is sculpted using the planar sculpting technique:**
   - » Panel 1 is sculpted first, followed by Panel 2 and Panel 3

4. **Sculpt Panel 1 using planar sculpting technique:**
   - » Distribute and project hair straight up from horizontal partings
   - » Position fingers/shears horizontally (parallel to floor)
   - » Sculpt parallel to fingers
   - » Work from front hairline toward crown using horizontal partings and mobile design line

   ☐

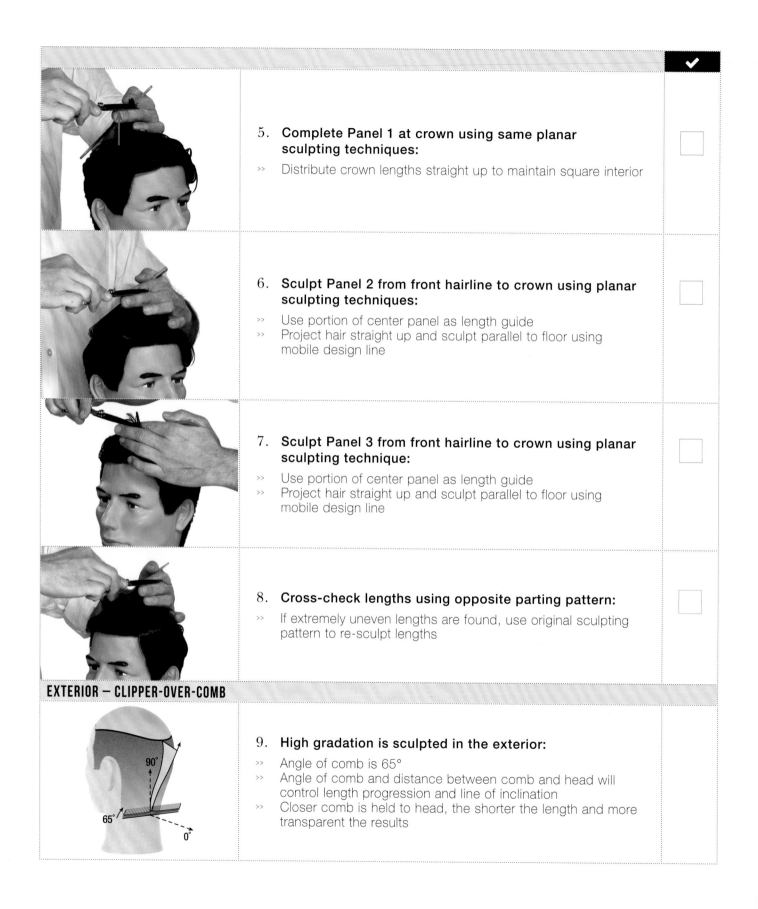

5. **Complete Panel 1 at crown using same planar sculpting techniques:**
   >> Distribute crown lengths straight up to maintain square interior

6. **Sculpt Panel 2 from front hairline to crown using planar sculpting techniques:**
   >> Use portion of center panel as length guide
   >> Project hair straight up and sculpt parallel to floor using mobile design line

7. **Sculpt Panel 3 from front hairline to crown using planar sculpting technique:**
   >> Use portion of center panel as length guide
   >> Project hair straight up and sculpt parallel to floor using mobile design line

8. **Cross-check lengths using opposite parting pattern:**
   >> If extremely uneven lengths are found, use original sculpting pattern to re-sculpt lengths

EXTERIOR – CLIPPER-OVER-COMB

9. **High gradation is sculpted in the exterior:**
   >> Angle of comb is 65°
   >> Angle of comb and distance between comb and head will control length progression and line of inclination
   >> Closer comb is held to head, the shorter the length and more transparent the results

10. Sculpt high line of inclination from center nape moving upward toward interior:

>> Position head upright
>> Use fine teeth of large comb (Master Sketcher)
>> Project hair at 90°
>> Angle comb at 65° to head
>> Control angle of comb with your thumb and index finger
>> Sculpt across comb with clippers

Note: Remember to flip comb and redistribute hair each time you sculpt.

11. Work upward maintaining a high line of inclination using clipper-over-comb technique.

12. Work from center toward left side using clipper-over-comb technique:

>> Angle comb along intended line of inclination
>> Work from hairline upward toward interior
>> Sculpt horizontally across comb
>> Adjust position of comb from horizontal to diagonal as needed as you work around curve of head

13. Sculpt left side beginning at perimeter of sideburn area:

>> Use same line of inclination as back

14. Angle comb slightly to blend side to back lengths:

>> Continue to sculpt across comb and adjust angle of comb as needed to blend lengths

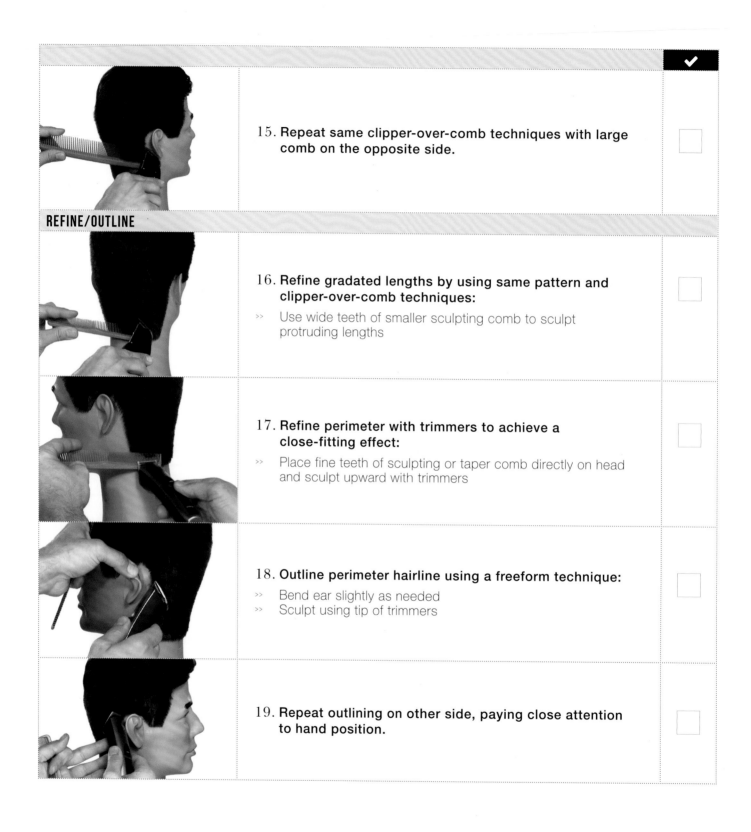

15. **Repeat same clipper-over-comb techniques with large comb on the opposite side.**

REFINE/OUTLINE

16. **Refine gradated lengths by using same pattern and clipper-over-comb techniques:**
    - >> Use wide teeth of smaller sculpting comb to sculpt protruding lengths

17. **Refine perimeter with trimmers to achieve a close-fitting effect:**
    - >> Place fine teeth of sculpting or taper comb directly on head and sculpt upward with trimmers

18. **Outline perimeter hairline using a freeform technique:**
    - >> Bend ear slightly as needed
    - >> Sculpt using tip of trimmers

19. **Repeat outlining on other side, paying close attention to hand position.**

TEXTURIZE ✔

20. **The interior lengths are texturized using the end-tapering technique with taper shears.**

21. **Project hair straight up, insert taper shears into ends of hair and close shears:**
    >> Continue process throughout interior
    >> Repeat where hair is dense or more end taper is desired

22. **The finish shows a strong square form that is well-suited to many men's facial features.**

COMPLETION

>> Discard single-use supplies
>> Disinfect tools and multi-use supplies
>> Disinfect workstation and arrange in proper order

20 mins
Suggested
Salon Speed

My Speed
_____
_____
_____

INSTRUCTIONS:
Record your time in comparison with the suggested salon speed. To improve my performance, I need to:

_____
_____
_____
_____
_____

BALD FADE
CLIPPERS

EXPLORE

All things that fade have a smooth transition. Describe something that fades.

INSPIRE

Visualize the result, follow a plan and with practice, you will achieve well-blended fades.

ACHIEVE

Following this *Bald Fade, Clippers Workshop,* you'll be able to:

» Explain how the hair is subdivided into zones prior to sculpting a bald fade

» Create a bald fade using clippers

This sculpture features gradation that smoothly blends into the skin.

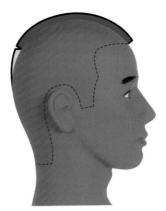

Lengths progress from near-bald at the hairline to high gradation toward the crest. Gradation blends to short, uniform lengths in the interior.

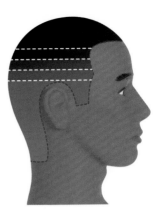

Five zones are used to create a smooth progression of lengths from the nape to the interior.

SCULPTING PROCEDURES

1. SECTION:
   (5) Zones

2. HEAD POSITION:
   Upright/Tilted forward

3. SCULPTING DIRECTION:
   Exterior: Upward
   Interior: Front hairline to crown

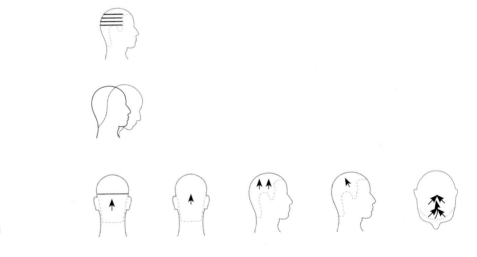

DESIGN DECISIONS CHART

BALD FADE CLIPPERS

Draw or fill in the boxes with the appropriate answers.

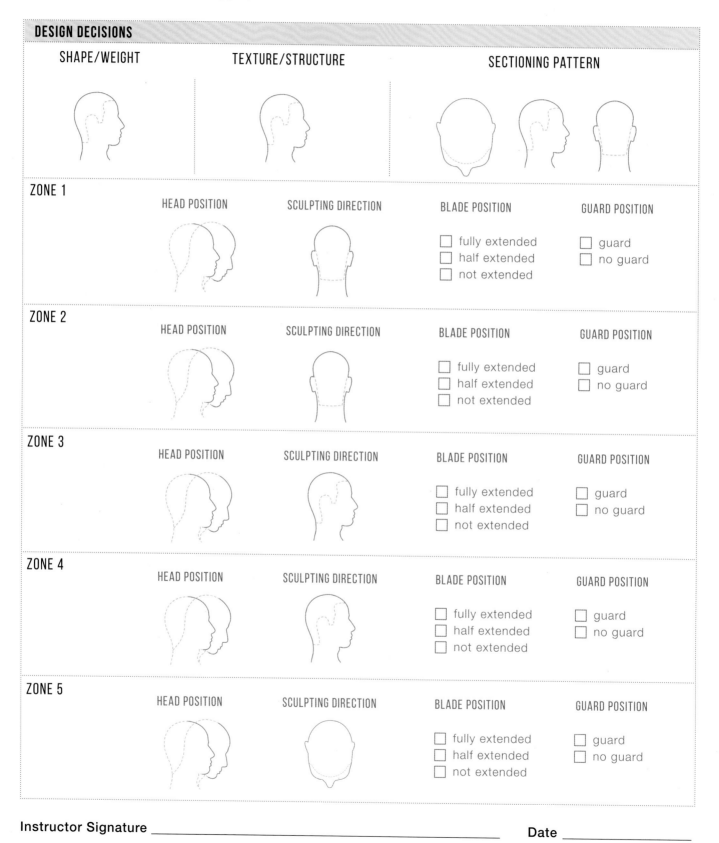

DESIGN DECISIONS

SHAPE/WEIGHT	TEXTURE/STRUCTURE	SECTIONING PATTERN

ZONE 1

HEAD POSITION	SCULPTING DIRECTION	BLADE POSITION	GUARD POSITION
		☐ fully extended ☐ half extended ☐ not extended	☐ guard ☐ no guard

ZONE 2

HEAD POSITION	SCULPTING DIRECTION	BLADE POSITION	GUARD POSITION
		☐ fully extended ☐ half extended ☐ not extended	☐ guard ☐ no guard

ZONE 3

HEAD POSITION	SCULPTING DIRECTION	BLADE POSITION	GUARD POSITION
		☐ fully extended ☐ half extended ☐ not extended	☐ guard ☐ no guard

ZONE 4

HEAD POSITION	SCULPTING DIRECTION	BLADE POSITION	GUARD POSITION
		☐ fully extended ☐ half extended ☐ not extended	☐ guard ☐ no guard

ZONE 5

HEAD POSITION	SCULPTING DIRECTION	BLADE POSITION	GUARD POSITION
		☐ fully extended ☐ half extended ☐ not extended	☐ guard ☐ no guard

Instructor Signature _____ **Date** _____

BALD FADE CLIPPERS

View the video, complete the Design Decisions chart, then perform this workshop. Complete the self-check as you progress through the workshop.

20
mins
Suggested
Salon Speed

PREPARATION	✔
>> Assemble tools and products >> Set up workstation	☐

SECTIONING	
1. Identify 5 zones: >> Number and width of each zone can vary depending on desired results	☐

ZONE 1	
2. Sculpt a horizontal line to establish position of Zone 1: >> Upright head position >> Place clippers flat on scalp; adjustable blade even with cutting blade >> Use outside of eyebrow as guide to establish line for Zone 1 >> Sculpt a horizontal line from front hairline to center back on both sides	☐
3. Check for symmetry of horizontal line.	☐
4. Sculpt Zone 1 against skin: >> Slightly forward head position >> Sculpt from center perimeter nape upward toward established horizontal line	☐

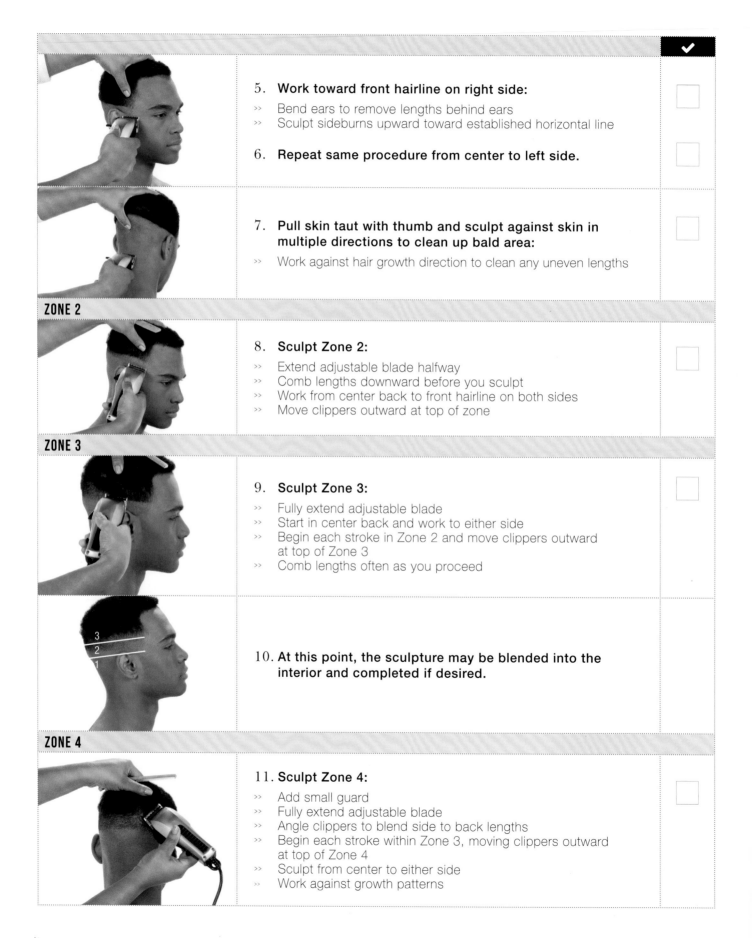

5. **Work toward front hairline on right side:**
   - >> Bend ears to remove lengths behind ears
   - >> Sculpt sideburns upward toward established horizontal line

6. **Repeat same procedure from center to left side.**

7. **Pull skin taut with thumb and sculpt against skin in multiple directions to clean up bald area:**
   - >> Work against hair growth direction to clean any uneven lengths

ZONE 2

8. **Sculpt Zone 2:**
   - >> Extend adjustable blade halfway
   - >> Comb lengths downward before you sculpt
   - >> Work from center back to front hairline on both sides
   - >> Move clippers outward at top of zone

ZONE 3

9. **Sculpt Zone 3:**
   - >> Fully extend adjustable blade
   - >> Start in center back and work to either side
   - >> Begin each stroke in Zone 2 and move clippers outward at top of Zone 3
   - >> Comb lengths often as you proceed

10. **At this point, the sculpture may be blended into the interior and completed if desired.**

ZONE 4

11. **Sculpt Zone 4:**
   - >> Add small guard
   - >> Fully extend adjustable blade
   - >> Angle clippers to blend side to back lengths
   - >> Begin each stroke within Zone 3, moving clippers outward at top of Zone 4
   - >> Sculpt from center to either side
   - >> Work against growth patterns

12. Sculpt uniform lengths in Zone 5:

>> Adjust blade even with cutting blade
>> Switch to a guard one size larger than previous
>> Comb hair forward prior to sculpting
>> Sculpt from center-front hairline to crown moving clippers against scalp
>> Work from center to right side, then from center to left side using same techniques
>> Move clippers in multiple directions against growth pattern

13. Sculpt crown and back to complete Zone 5.

BLEND ZONES

14. Blend Zones 1 and 2:

>> Position adjustable blade halfway; no guard
>> Pull skin taut and remove weight line
>> Use arcing motion moving away from head
>> Comb lengths
>> Work from center to each side

15. Blend Zones 2 and 3:

>> Fully extend adjustable blade; no guard
>> Remove weight line using same techniques
>> Work from center to each side

16. Blend Zones 3 and 4:

>> Extend lever halfway; smallest guard
>> Use same sculpting techniques

17. Blend Zones 4 and 5:

>> Fully extend adjustable blade; smallest guard
>> Use same sculpting techniques

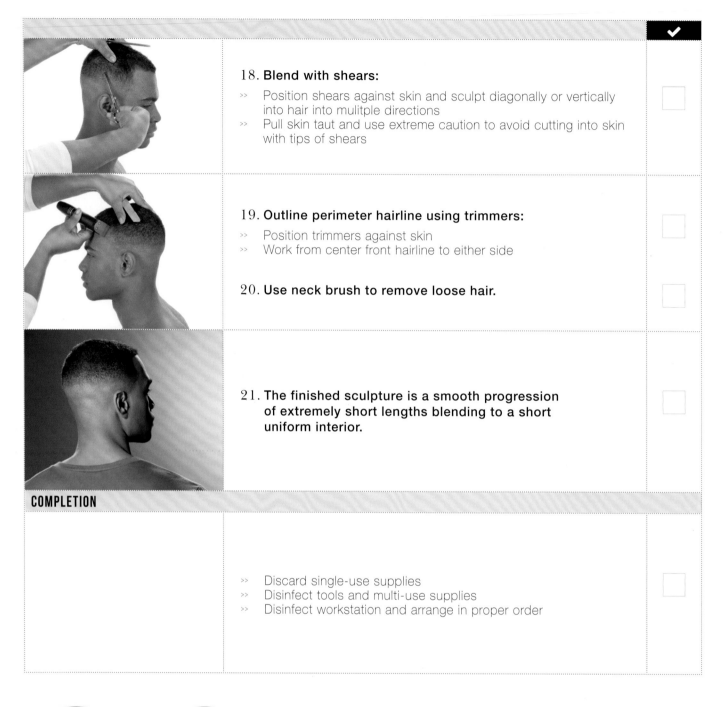

18. Blend with shears:

>> Position shears against skin and sculpt diagonally or vertically into hair into mulitple directions

>> Pull skin taut and use extreme caution to avoid cutting into skin with tips of shears

19. Outline perimeter hairline using trimmers:

>> Position trimmers against skin

>> Work from center front hairline to either side

20. Use neck brush to remove loose hair.

21. The finished sculpture is a smooth progression of extremely short lengths blending to a short uniform interior.

COMPLETION

>> Discard single-use supplies

>> Disinfect tools and multi-use supplies

>> Disinfect workstation and arrange in proper order

20 mins
Suggested
Salon Speed

INSTRUCTIONS:

Record your time in comparison with the suggested salon speed. To improve my performance, I need to:

_____

_____

_____

_____

≫106^c GLOSSARY/INDEX

*Term is found in 105.

PIVOT POINT

ACKNOWLEDGMENTS

Pivot Point Fundamentals is designed to provide education to undergraduate students to help prepare them for licensure and an entry-level position in the cosmetology field. An undertaking of this magnitude requires the expertise and cooperation of many people who are experts in their field. Pivot Point takes pride in our internal team of educators who develop cosmetology, esthetics and nails education, along with our print and digital experts, designers, editors, illustrators and video producers. Pivot Point would like to express our many thanks to these talented individuals who have devoted themselves to the business of beauty, lifelong learning and especially for help raising the bar for future professionals in our industry.

EDUCATION DEVELOPMENT — Janet Fisher // Sabine Held-Perez // Vasiliki A. Stavrakis
Markel Artwell
Eileen Dubelbeis
Brian Fallon
Melissa Holmes
Lisa Luppino
Paul Suttles
Amy Gallagher
Lisa Kersting
Jamie Nabielec
Vic Piccolotto
Ericka Thelin
Jane Wegner

EDITORIAL — Maureen Spurr // Wm. Bullion // Deidre Glover
Liz Bagby
Jack Bernin
Lori Chapman

DESIGN & PRODUCTION — Jennifer Eckstein // Rick Russell // Danya Shaikh
Joanna Jakubowicz
Denise Podlin
Annette Baase
Agnieszka Hansen
Kristine Palmer
Tiffany Wu

PROJECT MANAGEMENT — Jenny Allen // Ken Wegrzyn

DIGITAL DEVELOPMENT — John Bernin
Javed Fouch
Anna Fehr
Matt McCarthy
Marcia Noriega
Corey Passage
Herb Potzus

Pivot Point also wishes to take this opportunity to acknowledge the many contributors and product concept testers who helped make this program possible.

INDUSTRY CONTRIBUTORS

Linda Burmeister
Esthetics

**Jeanne Braa Foster,
Dr. Dean Foster**
Eyes on Cancer

Mandy Gross
Nails

Andrea D. Kelly, MA, MSW
University of Delaware

Rosanne Kinley
*Infection Control
National Interstate Council*

Lynn Maestro
Cirépil by Perron Rigot, Paris

Andrzej Matracki
*World and European
Men's Champion*

MODERN SALON

Rachel Molepske
*Look Good Feel Better, PBA
CUT IT OUT, PBA*

Peggy Moon
Liaison to Regulatory and Testing

Robert Richards
Fashion Illustrations

Clif St. Germain, Ph.D
Educational Consultant

Andis Company

International Dermal Institute

HairUWear Inc.

Lock & Loaded Men's Grooming

PRODUCT CONCEPT TESTING

**Central Carolina
Community College**
Millington, North Carolina

Gateway Community Colleges
Phoenix, Arizona

MC College
Edmonton, Alberta

Metro Beauty Academy
Allentown, Pennsylvania

**Rowan Cabarrus Community
College**
Kannapolis, North Carolina

**Sunstate Academy of
Cosmetology and Massage**
Ft. Myers, Florida

Summit Salon Academy
Kokomo, Indiana

TONI&GUY Hairdressing Academy
*Costa Mesa, California
Plano, Texas*

Xenon Academy
*Omaha, NE
Grand Island, NE*

LEADERSHIP TEAM

Robert Passage
Chairman and CEO

Robert J. Sieh
*Senior Vice President,
Finance and Operations*

Judy Rambert
Vice President, Education

Kevin Cameron
*Senior Vice President,
Education and Marketing*

R.W. Miller
*Vice President, Domestic Sales
and Field Education*

Jan Laan
*Vice President, International
Business Development*

Katy O'Mahony
Director, Human Resources

In addition, we give special thanks to the North American Regulating agencies whose careful work protects us as well as our clients, enhancing the high quality of our work. These agencies include Occupational Health and Safety Agency (OSHA) and the U.S. Environmental Protection Agency (EPA). *Pivot Point Fundamentals*™ promotes use of their policies and procedures.

Pivot Point International would like to express our SPECIAL THANKS to the inspired visual artisans of Creative Commons, without whose talents this book of beauty would not be possible.